IT'S MY LIFE!

1960S NEWCASTLE

Memories from people who were there

Edited by Anna Flowers and Vanessa Histon

Tyne Bridge Publishing

Tyne Bridge Publishing would like to express their very grateful thanks to all our contributors, who gave so generously of their time, memories and photographs. We were not able to include everything that was sent to us, but we hope that what is contained in the following pages gives a flavour of 1960s Newcastle.

Special thanks to ncjMedia and Tyne & Wear Archives & Museums for their evocative photographs.

We would also like to thank our printers, Elanders UK Ltd for their generous support in the production of this book.

Unless otherwise indicated illustrations are from the collections, and copyright of, Newcastle Libraries.

The views expressed in *It's My Life* are solely those of the contributors and in no way reflect the views of Tyne Bridge Publishing or the Council of the City of Newcastle upon Tyne.

Take a look at the **1960s Newcastle Timeline** on our website: **www.tynebridgepublishing.co.uk**

Cover design by **Stadt**

©Tyne Bridge Publishing, 2009; revised reprint, 2010

Published by
City of Newcastle upon Tyne
Newcastle Libraries & Information Service
Tyne Bridge Publishing, 2009

www.tynebridgepublishing.co.uk

www.newcastle.gov.uk/libraries

ISBN 978 185795 138 7

Printed by Elanders UK Ltd, North Tyneside

Opposite, student rag stunt, Blackett Street, 1963 (ncjMedia).

THE SWINGING SIXTIES

To those of us who grew up in them, the 1960s were extraordinary. It was the decade when, in Prime Minister Harold MacMillan's memorable phrase, we 'never had it so good' – not totally accurate, but an enduring idea. It was possible, as the sixties began, for the young to look ahead with confidence to a life which would offer work and excitement. Everything was possible and everything was changing. The remnants of Empire were fading fast, yet it was probably the last decade in which Britain had a clearly defined identity of its own. Europe still began on the other side of the Channel. We drove British-made cars. We watched British-made programmes on British-made televisions, wore British-made clothes. We knew who we were. It was a decade of confidence.

Above all it was the decade of the young. We were children of the Welfare State. We had been kept healthy by it and, above all, were educated by it. For the brightest, the grammar schools gave a high standard of education, even if they did divorce many from their origins in a country still sharply divided by class. It offered us work and a place in society.

It was the decade that created teenagers. They had certainly existed in the fifties, but nobody acknowledged them apart from blaming them for the excesses of the early Rock and Roll years. In the sixties, they came into their own and would be targeted by the world of commerce which provided the clothes and entertainment which still further defined them. The contraceptive pill, when it appeared, offered the young a sexual freedom that earlier generations were denied.

The Beatles and the other groups which appeared at the same time gave the young a voice. Bob Dylan, and others gave them a vision. Political awareness grew with the knowledge that the young could, perhaps, influence events. Involvement in protest groups – most notably the Campaign for Nuclear Disarmament – grew. It was the decade of the demonstration. Students were a minority, but they were the peer group leaders whose actions were admired by those not prepared to act themselves. For young women, the works of Germaine Greer and Betty Freidan made them aware that they need not be second-class citizens in a male-dominated world.

In Newcastle the 1960s opened with the heightened expectations commonly present at the dawn of a new decade but the city arrived in the 60s as it had left the 50s. The A1 was still the North Road and still Great, taking both local and through traffic slap through the middle of the city centre via

Opposite, Beryl Brydon at the New Orleans Club, early 1960s (Jim Perry).

'PENNY IN THE TUB'
ABOARD
BELLE
WILD BILL
CONCERT
NEWPORT YOUTH BAND
NEWPORT

Northumberland Street. By the end of the decade someone had thought to throw a temporary footbridge across the road but before that crossing between Fenwick's and Callers could be an exhilarating experience. Newcastle still had the Town Hall with which it had arrived in the 20th century, an age-blackened, colonnaded, neo-classical hulk at the divides of the Groat and Bigg Markets.

The only major problem was the threat of unemployment. In October 1959 it was announced that mining manpower was to be slashed and the Durham Coalfield, which had been 14,000 strong after the Second World War, had nearly halved its workforce by 1963. By 1967 the combined workforce of Northumberland, Durham and Cumberland was only 75,000. Suddenly, with more pit closures forecast, the future started to look bleak for many middle-aged men. The leader of Newcastle's Labour controlled City Council, T. Dan Smith, summed up the impact on the region's economy with his usual gritty eloquence at a meeting of the Northern Economic Planning Committee. 'Suddenly a bloody great hole has opened up'.

For Newcastle's young in 1960 – still barely recognised as teenagers – the centre of the swirl of social activity was the Oxford Ballroom in New Bridge Street. Girls in flared frocks which reached demurely to mid-calf and lads flaunting the tight trousers, draped jackets and Brylcreamed quiffs of the London Teddy Boys whose styles they aped, rocked and rolled to a band which was really much happier playing the 30s and 40s dance numbers of their mid-week repertoire.

In a world that seems now so wonderfully simple, there were no parking meters or betting shops to be seen. We spent pounds, shilling and pence, measured everything in feet and inches and weighed in stones, pounds and ounces. Upon these apparently solid foundations of a stable society, those determined to build a different future began their work. Some proposals were regional and would affect everybody in the North East.

The biggest of these was the 1963 Hailsham Plan's £50 million grant to provide the region and its capital with roads without parallel in Britain, incentives to new industries and new homes. It meant we would have new towns in Washington, Cramlington and Killingworth. Newcastle had plans of its own. Under its energetic planning boss Wilfred Burns, and prompted by politician T. Dan Smith's grandiose vision of creating a 'Brasilia of the North', a vast amount of finance was made available for redeveloping the city centre.

The process began in 1960 with the laying of the foundation stone for a new Civic Centre at Barras Bridge. The question of the location for a new headquarters for the City Council had been hotly debated for decades. At last, it was settled. When the Civic Centre finally opened, the old Town Hall became the site for exhibitions and indoor markets before being demolished.

Opposite, Haymarket, 1964. A trolley bus swings round towards Northumberland Street.

Taking the mood of its splendid new HQ, Newcastle City Council determined to be a market leader in local government. In 1965 T. Dan Smith appointed an industrialist from the motor industry to the job of Britain's first City Manager. Frank Harris was outspoken and determined, he trampled smartly on local government's corns as he cut red tape, as he had been hired to do, and filled the new Civic Centre with like-minded souls. The age of the civic mandarin dawned. With T. Dan Smith to urge them on – and give Newcastle a national figurehead – they planned, bulldozed and built. Amongst the losses was the classic 19th century Royal Arcade. It was pulled down to make way for the Swan House development – there were plans to re-erect it somewhere else, but the component parts were somehow lost.

The visible legacy of the 1960s included Eldon Square, the Central Library and the Central Motorway. T. Dan Smith himself barely lasted the decade he dominated. It had brought him success and honours. He became the *Architects' Journal*'s Man of the Year, was awarded an honorary degree from Newcastle University and was appointed chair of the Northern Economic Planning Council. In 1968 he was out of politics and devoting himself full time to his career as a public relations consultant. His friends and his own position in the corridors of power made him very popular with those businessmen intent on riding the development gravy train both in Newcastle and elsewhere.

In that year he was interviewed by the police in connection with his involvement in the affairs of the Borough of Wandsworth in London. He was cleared of offering bribes, but it was the start of his decline. He went on to face a number of corruption charges because of his close involvement with Yorkshire architect John Poulson in one of the biggest political scandals of the post-war period. Smith – tired, he claims of the whole business – pleaded guilty and was jailed. Until his death he insisted that he had never been found guilty of the charges he faced. He did, however, leave a stain on the reputation of the City of Newcastle.

Ordinary people in the sixties were only dimly aware of these political shenanigans. Their lives were changing in other, more important ways. Women's self-perception was about to undergo the most dramatic shift. Until the 1960s men were in control of sexual activity. They were the ones who had access to contraception. Then, came the Pill which gave women a sense of freedom they had not enjoyed before. The new attitude was summed up by a 19-year-old with the 'Cathy McGowan hairstyle' – shoulder length with a fringe – interviewed by the *Evening Chronicle* a few years after the Pill had arrived in Newcastle. 'This makes me the boss,' she said. 'That's all I'm going to say about it to you or anybody else'.

The *Lady Chatterley's Lover* trial in 1961 edged the country closer to a new, more open sexual attitude. Penguin Books were found not guilty of obscenity for publishing D.H. Lawrence's novel and bookshops in Newcastle ran out after one day, even though purchasers were rationed to just one copy

Opposite, Balmbra's, Cloth Market, 1964.

BALMBRA'S
Blaydon Bar
Music Hall & Buffet
Jubilee MILK STOUT
CARLING'S LAGER BEER

each. Sex became something to be discussed – and enjoyed.

For the young and the single there was, initially at least, no Pill – it was for married women only. The lack of easy availability of effective contraception was reflected in the continuing high rates of illegitimacy. Nationally, it was reckoned that one in five teenage girls was pregnant on her wedding day. When the sixties arrived, they were the first generation which 'had it all' – and they wanted more. 'Dolly Birds' with their styled hair, short skirts and heavy mascara expected to do what they wanted to do with their own lives, and that included their own bodies. But it was not until 1968 when the Pill became comparatively widely available on Tyneside that Newcastle women joined in the sexual revolution. 1967 saw abortion law reform but as the Pill became more widely available, so the need for abortions was reduced. The Pill became an accepted part of life. The teenager with the trendy hairdo who had proclaimed her sexual independence so emphatically to the *Evening Chronicle* reporter was one of many who led the way on a path which soon led to the use of the term 'permissive society' – it wasn't a pejorative description then.

Another development in 1967 confirmed the reality of the new tag. The law decriminalised homosexual acts between consenting adults in private. A leading homosexual rights activist in Newcastle – and few then were prepared to be so recognised – welcomed the move as the start of a new era. 'Now that we can behave the way we want in private, it will not belong before we have public acceptance', he said. 'In a few years time, people will not turn a hair when they see us holding hands and even kissing in public. By the middle of the next decade, we will be getting married just like heterosexuals'.

The 1960s was the decade when British pop music came of age and went on to conquer the world. 1950s Rock and Roll had produced its own youth culture but it did not embrace a whole generation. One phenomenon which would sweep the nation arrived in Newcastle on January 28, 1963, in the shaggy haired form of the Beatles. Pre-gig excitement was enthusiastic and teenagers queued from Friday afternoon until the tickets went on sale on Sunday for the concert at the Majestic Ballroom. The reaction to the band was extraordinary – Tyneside hadn't seen anything like the head shaking, shrieking frenzy which greeted the smartly dressed 'Fab Four' as soon as they went on stage.

The group – nobody called them a band at the time – were back at the Majestic in June that year, and Newcastle found a place in Beatle mythology. While staying at the Imperial Hotel on Jesmond Road, they wrote *She Loves You* which went on to become the biggest selling disc in British recording history. John, Paul, George and Ringo were back later on that year for the appearance which really marked their arrival at the top of the pop tree. Newcastle City Hall was one of the country's top venues. Four thousand fans queued in the December cold for 48 hours to get tickets and worried parents prompted the police to

Opposite, the Green Market, Newgate Street, just before it closed, 1970.

mount 'chastity patrols' of the queue to see that nothing untoward happened. 1963 and 1964 were the Beatles' glory years. The following year they were back at the City Hall for what was to be their final appearance in the North East, and in fact one of their last concerts. Once again the City Hall was packed. Beatlemania reigned supreme. It was hard to hear the music because of the wall of noise from the stalls. A steady succession of fainting girls were carried out of the auditorium.

Tyneside was also producing its own pop heroes. The action focussed on a sweaty little club in Percy Street called the Club A 'Gogo. It consisted of two rooms above the canteen serving the adjoining bus station. It specialised in the earthier blues which the Rolling Stones had made a rival to the melodically engineered pop songs of the Merseyside beat groups. In 1963, self-taught pianist Alan Price transferred his Alan Price Combo from the Downbeat Club in Carliol Square, not far away from the A 'Gogo. They were a bunch of working-class Tyneside youngsters who found that the blues admirably suited their style, especially the singer Eric Burdon, a gravel voiced, ruddy faced Electricity Board draughtsman.

The Animals became the house band of the A 'Gogo. But in 1964 and the lights of London beckoned and The Animals moved south, and became famous. They took America by storm the same year. 'Fab and getting fabber and fabber', enthused one New York writer. The accent intrigued the Americans. Tyneside became nearly as famous as Merseyside – The Animals' version of the blues classic *House of the Rising Sun* went global. For a brief spell in the sixties there was talk of the Geordie Sound. It didn't last long. When the Animals left, they were followed at the Club A 'Gogo by the Junco Partners who performed similar music in a different style, but while they were a success they never quite matched The Animals' fame and Tyneside did not produce the stream of groups which made Liverpool so distinctive.

The 'Swinging Sixties' marked the beginning of different attitudes, life style and even ways of thinking. For Newcastle and Tyneside, and Great Britain as a whole, things would never be quite the same again.

Dick Godfrey, retired Chief Feature Writer, the Journal, Newcastle
(Adapted from Tyne Bridge Publishing's 'Water Under the Bridges', 2000)

Opposite, Grainger Street, 1960.

Beatles fans, 1964 (ncjMedia).

THE KIDS ARE ALL RIGHT

Mik Richardson

Heaton Grammar School, mid-1960s.

Treats for the kids

I was the youngest of four and we lived in a large council house in what is now Cruddas Park. Believe it or not that was a desirable address in the sixties. Builders, dentists and doctors lived in our street. My father was a typical working-class man who did everything he could to ensure his children were raised to a higher standard than he was.

Dad worked at what was lovingly referred to as 'The Bone Yard', a glue factory in Walker. Each week the men had money deducted from their pay packet so that every Christmas we had a trip to the panto and every summer a day out in a 'charabanc' to the seaside or the countryside.

We met at the factory which had the most awful smell I have ever encountered in my life, but we always arrived with great anticipation and expectation. We were special because our dads worked in that place, doing what I didn't know, but if it was my dad it had to be very important. My sister, brothers and myself were extra special because not only did my dad work there but my aunt was the manageress of the staff canteen – very very important.

We only had coal fires then, no such thing as radiators. We used blankets not duvets and bedrooms were shared. Two shillings pocket money a week got us into the local pictures, a sixpenny mix-up and sixpence left over to spend through the week or, as we were made to do, save via school into the Trustee Savings Bank.

We played in the streets, with skipping ropes, balls and our imaginations. We were out as late as we were allowed to be and people looked out for each other's children. The doors were not often locked and we were never allowed our own key.

Pam Wilson

Newcastle kids at play around 1960.

Byker memories

Christmas was something that was saved for, at the grocer's, butcher's or even the newsagent's. Mam was paid weekly and every week a few pennies were saved in these savings clubs. It was a way of guaranteeing some luxuries at Christmas time and it was exciting getting the toy catalogue that the newsagent supplied every year and dreaming of what Santa might bring. My fondest Christmas memory is of getting a roll top desk and a portable typewriter bought with a 'ticket' from Parrish's on Shields Road.

Parrish's, Shields Road, Byker, 1964. Raby Street stretches beyond.

Christmas parties were great if your dad was a member of The Middle or The Bottom Club (Working Men's Social Clubs) on Raby Street. These were great events and l remember getting some super presents from Santa who seemed to vary in weight from one year to the next! If you had an Aunty that worked at the Domestos factory like I did, you got invited to their Christmas 'do' which was often held at the Apollo Cinema at the bottom of Shields Road. Not only did you get to see a great film, you got a goodie bag with sweets to eat whilst you watched the film, and as you left you got a present from Santa himself! Boy was I a lucky girl getting to go to both.

Trips to the coast were a mammoth undertaking, as well as the five of us (Mam, Dad, me and two brothers), there would be the rest of the family including gran, grandad, uncles, aunties, cousins and neighbours. We all had to sit with the deck chairs forming a circle with the smaller kids sitting in the middle on towels. The men all wore their suits and in the afternoon they all went 'missing' but when they all came back they always seemed to be in 'better spirits' and if they remembered we all got little twists of chips on their return. Even if it rained we still went to the beach. Once it was organised not even the rain could put us off. If it was cold we took flasks of Heinz vegetable soup to warm us up but we still used to go for plodges, even in the rain. The smell of Diesel still reminds me of those trips to the seaside and waiting at Heaton Station for the next train.

Easter was a lovely time. Nearly everyone got a new outfit or, if money was tight, just a new hat. The shops used to be closed from the Thursday afternoon until the Tuesday morning – apart from the wet fish shop on the Good Friday; that used to do a roaring trade with queues that seemed to last forever. The fish shop that we used was only about 100 yards from our house, so we used to take turns in waiting in the queue – no one liked fish in our house but on that day we had to have it! We couldn't buy it days in advance then because there weren't many people that had fridges. Bottles of milk used to be kept 'fresh' by standing them in buckets of cold water.

Not all memories are nice ones. Every so often I would come into the scullery to find a sheep's head steeping in a bucket – not a pleasant sight! Dad used to like the sheep's brains cooked and spread on his toast – not for the faint hearted. Mind I did like to suck on the pigs' trotters every so often!

Shawn Fairless

A very run-down Heaton Station, early 1970s.

Byker kids

The winters were much colder with lots of snow and when it came you sledged on the main roads! The best fun was weaving your way around the cars that had been abandoned, unable to move on the un-gritted roads. For the brave Byker lads, Avondale Road, the steepest and longest, was a must; the speed you achieved would win you an Olympic Gold – that's if you survived the No.19 bus and the brick wall at the bottom of Raby Street …

Avondale Road, 1966. A challenge for sledgers.

When it wasn't snowing, which seemed like only eight months of the year, you could always play ON the railway. The branch line closed at 7pm and, with a spanner and a little knowledge, you had a ticket to ride the manual 'push me, pull you' cart on the line. You just had to keep an eye out for the evening goods trains from Shepherds.

Grass cuttings in Harbottle Park gave us a day's entertainment with grass fights, competitions for the best dive into a colossal pile of grass and many more imaginative games. The grass was collected while 16-bladed open cutters whizzed past you, just inches away, showering you with a rain of grass.

Hot days would give us the opportunity to play with the most versatile material known to us Byker lads – tar. It could be moulded, burnt, used with lolly sticks to make sailing ships to launch on the 'clarts' beside Shepherds, or you could write on walls (and it dripped off on the next hot day). The only drawback was the smell of the butter that your mother used to take the stain from clothes, skin and hair … I can still smell it to this day!

Lolly sticks were also used to challenge your mates to see whose stick snapped the quickest or lasted the longest – similar to conkers. Five small cubes of wood became 'chucks', and endless entertainment.

Martin Fairless

My childhood memory of Byker is of a very friendly community, everyone was helpful and though no one had much, people shared. Everything seemed to happen in the back lane of Shipley Street. Myself, my brother Lance, our landlord's children and the rest of the 'street gang' played there while adults gossiped. We played football, cricket and darts, we had accidents but you had to brush yourself off and carry on. We had bonfires on Guy Fawkes, charring neighbours' back doors!

I went to Raby Street School from 1964 until 1972. Most of the buildings, including the infant block, have been demolished. The classrooms in the junior school were down two sides of the assembly hall with a stage at one end. Every morning as the teachers and children gathered for assembly and the headmaster, Mr Douglas, made his way to the lectern in front of the stage, the jolly, rotund, teacher, Mr McMahon, would play the accordion or a couple of the older juniors played a selection of classical and popular music on the reel-to reel-tape recorder at the side of the stage.

Brian Thompson

Heaton Park was, and still is, a place I love to visit – when I was young and my twin brother and sister were born, my mam and I used to hang onto the extra large Silver Cross twin pram as we went down the hill and then struggled to push it back up again. We had some great days there picnicking and just sitting out in the fresh air during the summer holidays.

At the bottom of the back lane on the corner, was a wet fish shop where my mam sent

Corbridge Street, Byker, 1962.

me to buy fish heads for the cat. I dreaded this, as no matter how I tried to convince the lady to wrap the heads up with lots of paper they always seemed to fall out and scatter all over the pavement with their eyes staring up at me. To this day I cannot pass a fishmongers without turning my head away from those eyes!

Worse still was the butcher's shop at the top of Shields Road where we'd buy a sheep's head for broth – guess who had to carry it home in newspaper! I used to run all the way home, praying the head would not soak through the paper and drop out. One day it did. I know it fell out somewhere but I never went back to look for it. I was in so much trouble when I got back for wasting money – I got no tea that night, I must have been nine or ten.

When I was about 11 or 12, I went to dancing classes at a studio called The Silver Swing at the bottom of Shields Road, past the Apollo cinema. Saturday morning from 10-12 was ballroom dancing. Susan, my friend, was a year younger but she had been going for some time and was very good at it. Even though I was new the instructor kept me with Susan, but I had the male role of leading and I am sure, that's why I can't dance properly – I'm still leading! At the end of the session they would play Chubby Checker's *Let's Twist Again*, which we thought was great.

Linda Gray

The Apollo, Shields Road, 1967.

Raby Street, Byker, 1970.

Raby Street

Raby Street was lined with local shops of all description, including the Co-op where butter was bought by the pound from a huge slab, not neatly packaged as it is today. Corner shops abounded, sweet shops were far more interesting and there were shops that don't even exist today, such as Meggie Rickard's snuff shop where my gran used to send me on messages to get small parcels wrapped in old newspaper.

Nick Rogerson

Summer holidays in Walker

Walker Library (how imposing it seemed!) provided constant entertainment in the school holidays. I was an avid reader and there were very few books in our house. My parents were Hongkong Chinese who came to Britain in the 1950s; they were not great readers themselves and had very little free time after working long hours in the catering trade. It didn't take long for me to exhaust the children's section, but when I told the librarian that I had read all the books there, apart from the ones that were too young for me, she took pity and gave me a 'grown up' ticket that allowed me to borrow from the adult section.

Grace Shaw (nee Wong)

The Winter Zoo

In the winter of 1969 the Old Town Hall, which used to stand at the bottom of the Bigg and Cloth Market, played host to a Winter Zoo. I remember the straw floored animal pens going down the sides of the hall. Lance and I had our photograph taken with a parrot on Lance's shoulder and me holding a monkey, and wearing woollen balaclavas which we were always made to wear in winter.

Brian Thompson

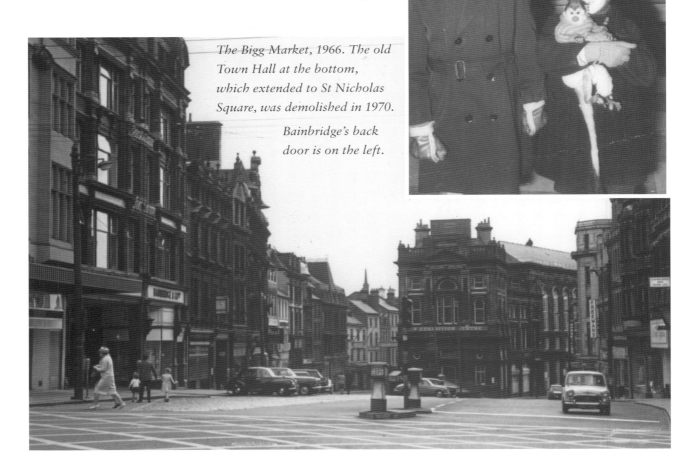

The Bigg Market, 1966. The old Town Hall at the bottom, which extended to St Nicholas Square, was demolished in 1970.

Bainbridge's back door is on the left.

The Valley

At the bottom of our street was 'The Valley'. Adults called it Blackies Valley. It used to be some kind of slag heap but it was filled in and a culvert put through the middle of it. This was our playground most of the time. There were trees for spears and bow and arrows and of course fires – we just loved fires. At the top were derelict wooden garages. We'd take the tarpaulin off the roofs, which would really get the fires going. For football we crossed the road to the Little Moor. The only problem was cows, or to be more precise, what they tended to deposit on the grass.

Another place for football was the back lane where we would play 'Doors'; you picked a back door which was your goal to defend and you had to score against other players' doors. This was OK up to a point but it sometimes didn't go down too well with some of the residents. I don't think anybody bothered us even if we came back home covered in mud, blood and smelling of smoke.

In our family you could tell what day of the week it was by what we had for dinner. There was always roast chicken on Saturdays after my mother had been down to the market in Newcastle to get a fresh one (we never had a fridge, freezer, washing machine or car during this time). Salads on summer Sundays and something made from leftover chicken and chicken soup on Mondays.

Mik Richardson

Mik Richardson

Blackies Valley, High West Jesmond, 1960s

nciMedia

'Mr Newcastle', T. Dan Smith, Chairman of the Housing Committee, hands over the keys to the new tenant of the 30,000th house on Newbiggin Hall Estate, 20 February, 1962.

Dan Smith became Leader of Newcastle City Council in 1960 and promised to rebuild Newcastle as the 'Brasilia of the North'. Many of the city's Victorian slums were swept away but the tower blocks that replaced them were often badly built and unpopular.

Opposite, Elswick, 1970 (Norman McCord).

My dream home

In 1962, I received a letter from the Town Hall asking me to collect a key for a council house in Newbiggin Hall Estate. Can you imagine my excitement after living in an upstairs flat with my mother for eight years? My son was eight years old and my daughter two years, I left the children with my mother – they had mumps at the time – and I remember thinking when I got off the bus that I was almost in the country with woods, fields and MY house!

I was amazed, living room, kitchen and three bedrooms, and, best of all, a bathroom. A bath with taps! At my mother's, we had a tin bath which hung in the scullery – it had to be filled and emptied once a week.

We moved in February and the weather was dreadful, very deep snow which hid the front path. It was quickly cleared and our small amount of furniture was carried in. We had no carpets, just rugs, but we were happy because we had our own house.

On the down side, there was no heating upstairs and because of that there would be Jack Frost on the inside of windows each morning. I was so cold I used to get dressed in bed. We had under-floor heating in the living room, which was very expensive to run but very handy for drying clothes.

I am now 75 years old and still here, so you could say I've had a good life in this house.

Susan Dixon

Vale House, Jesmond Vale, 1968. The 28-storey block contains 138 flats and cost £534,000 to build. In 1969 it won the Ministry of Housing and Local Government Award for Good Design.

From old to new. A series of photographs taken in 1962 to illustrate the move from an older house to a new council dwelling, from the signing of the tenancy agreement and the handing over of the new key, to the arrival in the modern kitchen.

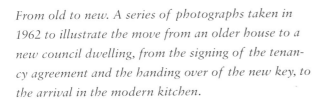

The L-Shaped Room

Of course I lived in a bed-sit, as did many of the inhabitants of Jesmond. I remember sitting on the grass outside the new Civic Centre, by the War Memorial, scouring the *Evening Chronicle* for somewhere to stay. I ended up in a house shared by 12 people and only one bathroom … which had a permanently wet floor, covered in burnt bits of newspaper (there was an Ascot heater). I took to washing in a plastic bowl, in front of my gas fire! My tiny kitchen was dirty, but I brightened it up by gloss-painting the walls peacock blue and the woodwork buttercup yellow. I also emulsioned the walls of my room (magnolia and sky blue) and stuck dried leaves on for an artistic effect. Nobody objected. The room was slightly damp, with silverfish living under the floor boards, the sash window was cracked and there was a hint of leaking gas. But it was home. To escape from the squalor, I used to walk down the road to Jesmond Dene on Sunday afternoons and sit on the grass in the sunshine with lots of other bed-sit dwellers.

Tyneside flats on Shortridge Terrace, Jesmond, late 1960s.

Another joy of Jesmond living was Mr Vedhara's shop, which always seemed to be open and gave me my first experience of Indian cooking.

Rose Reeve

I Can See for Miles

I was born on the 26th November 1960 and grew up in Shipley Street, Byker. We had a terraced flat with stone backstairs leading down to the yard and the outside toilet. Our landlord and his family lived in the downstairs flat. All of the terraced streets in Byker in the mid 60s were being demolished to be replaced by the Byker Wall and Village. Everywhere was a playground and as houses were being emptied and demolished we had another place to explore, as long as we didn't mind the risk of being told off by the bobby on the beat from Headlam Street station. As far as my parents were concerned, however, our neighbourhood was rapidly descending into slums. We were moved out of the terraces in 1966 into one of T. Dan Smith and John Poulson's 'visionary' tower blocks in Heaton.

I remember our move into the flats. The concierge greeted us at the entrance, giving a grander impression of the flats than they really deserved. We lived on the seventh floor. Even though we had only moved about a mile, our horizons had extended, we now had had new friends to make and Heaton Park and Jesmond Dene to explore. The most vivid memory I have of living in Molineux Court was highlighted by Peter Flannery in his TV series *Our Friends in the North*. The flats were freezing in winter, with a combination of concrete walls, aluminium single-glazed windows and no heating other than an electric fire in the living room. There was under-floor heating in the living room only, which we could not afford to run. Thick ice formed on the inside of the windows, condensation formed icicles, and a sweep of the hand across the walls came away soaking wet.

One compensation of living on the seventh floor of a tower block was the superb view along the Tyne valley. On the evening of on April 25th 1969, my mother was looking in the living room mirror, in which you could see Newcastle skyline reflected. Suddenly she shouted 'look there's a plane

The type of house that would be swept away, 1964.

crashing!' My brother and I ran to the window to see a flaming meteorite entering the atmosphere at about 40 degrees above the horizon. It travelled east to west along the Tyne valley causing sonic booms and seemed to come down in the west end of Newcastle. Of course it had travelled over the horizon and the larger of two chunks landed in Bovedy, Northern Ireland. Over its 310 mile trajectory it was visible from England, Wales and Ireland.

Brian Thompson

College blues

For the first three years of my course at Newcastle Art College I travelled in every day on the bus from Blyth. I wasn't given enough grant to be able to afford to live in a flat and I hated leaving college in the evenings; my friends would be going off to the pub or to parties and I would have to get the bus home. So for my final year I went to see the man at Northumberland County Council who gave out grants and made a bid to have mine increased. My argument was that I had so much extra work to do and was wasting two hours a day sitting on a bus when I could be

Heaton Park Court, 1967, built to the same design as Molineux.

slaving over a hot drawing board in a flat. He went for it, so I was then able to move into a flat on Sandyford Road right on the edge of Jesmond (where else?) and only a few minutes walk from college.

The flat was very cheap because it was earmarked to be pulled down in order to widen Sandyford Road. It stood where the mini roundabout is at the end of Osborne Terrace.

On one side was the Salvation Army office, we were above the betting shop and at the other side was the well known old fashioned grocer's shop Leathard's. There was another branch on St George's Terrace in Jesmond. They were fascinating shops with marble counters on top of which they kept the bacon slicers and big slabs of butter. There were hams

Geoff Laws' flat on Sandyford Road.

hanging from the ceiling and you could buy loose biscuits in paper bags. Unfortunately they couldn't compete in price with the supermarkets and disappeared in the 70s. Just to complete the picture there was an off-licence in the next block, which is still there under a different name, and we would sometimes scrape together what little change we had to buy a bottle of cider on a Sunday evening.

Behind the flat were the dilapidated terraces of Shieldfield, which were soon to be pulled down to make room for the Polytechnic campus and alongside was the railway line from Manors station which looped around north of the Tyne and pre-dated the Metro.

I spent the chilly winter of 1968-1969 at the flat but was finally able to live the complete student life.

Geoff Laws

I would walk to school through Jesmond Dene with my transistor and just disappeared into the music.

Mik Richardson

We would walk to Heaton Park on a Sunday afternoon to get to Jesmond Dene for 5pm. We took our small transistor radio and stopped just before the waterfall. We would sit in the shelter and listen to the top 20 with Jimmy Saville for an hour, and woe betide anyone who interrupted this ritual in our little sanctuary.

Linda Gray

For me the music of the sixties WAS the sixties and thank God I was there as a teenager to experience it all.

Margaret Dinsdale

There was tangible positive energy around during that period. All of us in the band were charged by it and we probably generated a considerable amount of our own … we really felt that our time was coming and things were changing for the better.

Ray Laidlaw

Opposite, Beatles fans, 1964 (ncjMedia).

I HEARD IT THROUGH THE GRAPEVINE

All that Jazz

What people don't realise is that outside London, Newcastle was probably the biggest centre for jazz in the country.

My neighbours were in a modern jazz group called the EMCEE Five. They used to rehearse in my house. I used to have a piano in those days and we set up the drum kit in the window. One of the founder members, Mike Carr, eventually went down to play at Ronnie Scott's club in London. Ian Carr, his brother left the EMCEE Five to found a band called The Nucleus. They gave it the horrible name Be-bop, which came from America. Ronnie Stephenson, the original drummer went to Johnnie Dankworth's club and ended up playing with Val Parnell. Ronnie was one of the foremost drummers in Europe, if not the world.

Jim Perry

My flat in Victoria Square was a bit of a haven for jazz musicians. I was a founder member of Jazz North East in the late 1950s and we put on jazz concerts in the old YMCA building. On the top floor was a lovely debating chamber that seated around 300 with a small grand piano which we had tuned. One of the first bands we put on was one of the all-time greats, Earl Hines with the Alex Welsh band. It was the best concert they did because we had a good piano. These big Americans like challenges.

Johnny Griffin, who had played with Thelonius Monk played at the YMCA with Mike Carr accompanying him. We met at the Eldon Grill for drinks first but Johnny wouldn't say just

Victoria Square, 1964 – a leafy haven for jazz fans.

The YMCA, Blackett Street, 1966. There was a lot going on there, from the coffee bar in the basement next door to the jazz on the top floor. The Eldon Grill was opposite, on the corner of Blackett Street and Grey Street.

what he was going to play. During the concert, without any warning, Johnny suddenly shouted 'Exactly!' and launched into an up-tempo version of 'Exactly like you', no indication of what key. Mike's hands were all over the keyboard and it was a wonderful night. Mike always played in a bluesy style. We had Bill Coleman, Benny Webster, Edmund Hall, who played with Louis Armstrong, and Ted Wilson who was a member of Benny Goodman's band. Newcastle was a Mecca for jazz. Musicians used to say that outside London the best reception they got was in Manchester or Newcastle.

Count Basie's brass section in full flight at the City Hall.

Mike Jeffery was an enigmatic figure, with shady connections, but he encouraged jazz in Newcastle by opening jazz clubs. The Downbeat off Carliol Square was one of the first. It was pretty basic (Mike was tight with his money!), up a long stairway, with an old piano on the stage. That was where I first met Alan Price. Here was this guy playing wonderful bluesy piano. I invited him and his girlfriend back to my flat. Eric Burdon came back with him one night and I put on *Security Blues* by Roosevelt Sax. Eric lay on the floor with his ear practically

Alan Price on Percy Street, 1960s.

inside the speaker!

Alan Price came to live in Victoria Square for a while. He was touring with the Animals and he got fed up – there were arguments within the band as there often are, and Alan just left. We tried to get him down to the Central Station and make him get onto a train to rejoin the band for the next stage of the tour but he'd had enough, 'I'm packing it in', he said. So he stayed with us and formed the Alan Price Set. Marcus Price (no relation) fitted them all out with cheap shiny imitation mohair suits as bands wore at the time. Alan persuaded John Walters (later John Peel's producer),

The Downbeat Club in the early 1960s.

who lived in the flat downstairs to be a member and give up his job at Kenton School. John also played trumpet with Mighty Joe Young's Jazz Band. Alan slept in my flat and he ate in John's flat. The pile of dirty shirts that accumulated in my flat was Alan's. There must have been 20 or 30. He just went out and bought new ones. Later on Radio Newcastle asked me to do a jazz programme which I did for a few years. I interviewed musicians like Cathy Stobart, Ronnie Scott and Stefan Grapelli.

David Bell

The New Orleans Club

Cross Byker Bridge heading east, then drop sharp right down decaying Melbourne Street. Stop, now listen. On certain nights you would became slowly aware of a distant rhythmic, almost mechanical beat, the source of which was at first obscure. Further on a handful of people could be seen queuing at a doorway and then you would hear the soaring wail of a jazz trumpet, to me, then as now, the most exciting of all musical sounds.

With increasing apprehension we paid our money. We were in the New Orleans Club, which we attended regularly, three nights a week, during my university holidays from 1958 and into the sixties.

The New Orleans Club photographed in the early 1960s by Jim Perry. 'The floor used to go thump thump thump and when you looked down there was just a long vista of brown ale bottles! You were squashed together! (Pauline Luke)

As with so many clubs, there was a smoky upstairs room with blackened windows, a bar, and a small stage decorated with grubby posters. Notable was a faux music hall bill headed by Long John Baldry with several others.

The Club was open seven nights a week. Then, as now, hyperbole was happily accepted. Mighty Joe Young was in life a small man fronting a large band. Ronnie Mclean the trombonist played traditional jazz with a passion. There was Big Pete Deuchar, of brewery fame and Sheila Giles (Lizzie from New Orleans) and her band.

Alan Price played occasional piano before the Animals formed. For us, Eric Burdon was the most original. Besides singing he would cup his hands and play a trumpet mouthpiece, sounding, at least in hindsight, exactly like the real thing. Newcastle Breweries' products were favoured by the men, with Babycham, Cherry B (Knicker Droppers) and Gin and Tonic for the ladies.

We would have to leave as the session accelerated to a climax in order to catch the last train. The city pubs closed at 10pm until 1962, when opening was extended to 10.30. Fifteen minutes before, crowds would throng the streets desperate for a last drink or two at a different location. When my girlfriend acquired an Austin 7 we would go to the Golden Palace for prawn fried rice or to sample the increasingly cosmopolitan takeaway of the Chip Shop on Westgate Road.

Inevitably Byker was developed. Though the establishment moved to Forth Banks, it was never quite the same.

Guy Hall

An Animal's tale

Eric Burdon and I met in our first year of art college in 1956. We were both school dropouts and we shared an enthusiasm for jazz, rock 'n' roll and (mainly American) movies and books.

Early in 1957 we started a band called the Pagan Jazzmen with Eric on trombone, me on trumpet, Jimmy Crawford on banjo and Alan Sanderson on drums. By 1958 everyone was into rhythm and blues so we reformed as the Pagans with Eric on vocals/guitar, Alan on bass guitar, me on drums and Dave Ashcroft on rhythm guitar and piano. We met Alan Price in March 1959 when we played at a gig in a church hall in Byker. The other band playing that night was the Frank Hedley Quartet (they played pure Jerry Lee Lewis numbers). Their guitarist sat in with us playing the church hall's old upright piano – that was Alan Price. He joined the Pagans and over the next couple of years we went through various changes of name and line-up, all based around Eric, Alan and me. As the Kansas City Five and Kansas City Seven we played the New Orleans Club and The Downbeat for whatever we could get on the door. Alan was poached by the Kon-Tors in May 1962 and met Chas Chandler who was their bass guitarist. That was the end of the Pagans.

After that I got casual work, playing in working men's clubs, gaming clubs and at weddings. Eventually I got a professional residency at Emerson's (in Emerson Chambers). It was Newcastle's first steakhouse and had a resident trio and cabaret and postage stamp-sized dance floor. One summer day in

1963 I bumped into Chas Chandler on Northumberland Street. He told me that Alan Price had formed a band with Chas on bass, Eric on vocals and Nigel Stanger on sax. They were getting a lot of gigs but weren't happy with their drummer, so Chas asked if I'd be interested in coming back to join them. I said I couldn't afford to

John Steel and Eric Burdon in the Kansas City Five at the Downbeat Club, around 1959.

– I was getting £15 a week at Emerson's. Chas floored me by saying that he was on about £14 a week because the band were doing so many gigs at the A 'Gogo, plus one at the Victoria in Whitley Bay, and a12-3am Saturday slot at the Downbeat (after playing the A 'Gogo from 8-10 or 11pm.) I decided I'd rather be playing music I enjoyed than sitting in a steakhouse playing smooth cocktail jazz.

My first gig with the Alan Price Rhythm and Blues Combo was on September 8th 1963. It was a late session at Downbeat and I was paid £3. I was gobsmacked – the place was jammed and the band had built up a great following – there seemed

The Kon-Tors record.

to be a completely new atmosphere that night. I was the first time I was introduced to Hilton Valentine – he had been brought in to replace Nigel who was going to university – and played with the line up that was to become the Animals.

Later that year the Graham Bond Organisation (Graham Bond, Jack Bruce, Ginger Baker and Dick Heckstall-Smith) played the A 'Gogo. Graham suggested we should be called something snappier than the Alan Price Rhythm and Blues Combo – what about the Animals? He also got Mike Jeffery, our manager, interested in having a look at the London scene. Graham introduced Mike to Giorgio Gomolsky (original

Jim Perry

The Alan Price Combo – Chas Chandler, Eric Burdon, Nigel Stanger and Alan Price, plus drummer, around 1962.

manager of Rolling Stones, but managing the Yardbirds at the time) and Ronan O'Reilly (who owned the Scene Club and founded Radio Caroline). Mike came back to Newcastle with a deal whereby the Yardbirds would come to the North East and do our gigs for about 10 days while we went down to London and did the Yardbirds' gigs. The gigs in London were a success and on January 2, 1964 we all moved down to the big city. We were different from most northern groups because we had a jazz background so in London we made our mark from the off.

Our first gig at Newcastle City Hall was with the Chuck Berry tour on 23rd May 1964. It was the first time Chuck had toured Europe. We kicked off in London and The Swinging Blue Jeans got booed off because they were Liverpool pop and the front row at all of the shows was always full of rockers so their music was wrong for the audiences we drew. We were promoted to second on the bill.

We recorded House of the Rising Sun in one take during that tour. We finished our spot in Liverpool on the 17th, drove down to London, recorded the song and a 'B' side and then went on to Southampton to pick up the tour on 18th.

The Newcastle show was on the 23rd and we arrived home by train. There was a seething mob outside Central Station and we just didn't know how to handle it! I had a case in each hand and the police had to join hands around me and push me back inside for safety. Hilton got his suit torn and turned up later at the A 'Gogo all

Above, the Animals play the City Hall in 1964, and below, less than a year later, they were headlining the Kinks. (Advertisements from Newcastle Evening Chronicle.)

Eric Burdon and John Steel enjoy the return to Newcastle with a pint or two at the Northumberland Arms, 23 May 1964.

scratched to bits with his suit in shreds. Eric just took one look at the crowd, turned round and ran right back into the station, found a train to the coast, got off at Walker and went home. The police got me into a car and we went to the A 'Gogo, things quietened down and I eventually got home. We played at the City Hall four or five times.

While we were in still living in Newcastle there was a tour with the Everly Brothers headlining, and Bo Diddley plus a new band called The Rolling Stones. We went to the Odeon to see them, but we had to walk out just before Everly Brothers came on. It was really embarrassing as everyone knew who we were, but we had to get to the A 'Gogo in time for our set. Later Mike invited everyone back to the A 'Gogo and the Rolling Stones jammed in the Jazz Lounge though they never played there officially as far as I can recall (they had previously played in the Young Set).

By the time Ann (my wife) and I came back to Newcastle at the end of 1966 psychedelia was gradually percolating north from London. I opened a shop in partnership with childhood friend Bob Clennell – a boutique called Target in Handyside Arcade. I also played weekends in the restaurant at the new Newcastle Airport. It was considered the height of sophistication to dine on roast pheasant while watching the occasional aircraft take off for Manchester or Glasgow.

When the band broke up I came back to Newcastle and lived in Jesmond. We did a reunion show at City Hall in 1968 when Chas asked if I'd join his management and production company, I moved back to London in 1969. I still kept playing in bands in London.

Bruce Springsteen said our recording of 'It's My Life' was what encouraged him to make a career in music.

John Steel

A year of fame

On 20 February 1965 Maureen Cleave's *Evening Chronicle Pop Spot* featured an interview with the Animals who had 'survived a year of fame'. She says: 'They still don't look too smart; their hair sticks out in funny places, and they wear torn khaki jackets and hand-knitted jerseys and orange shirts and purple shirts.'

Eric Burdon pictured in the Evening Chronicle, 20 February, 1965, in a sheepskin coat stitched by his sister.

ncjMedia

It was a scream

Who remembers the Rolling Stones coming to Newcastle in October 1965? Me! How could I forget? My friend Vivien and I camped out in the freezing cold for tickets all night. When I got the ticket I felt like I'd won the golden ticket in *Charlie and the Chocolate Factory*, three rows from the front – 12s 6d. I couldn't wait to get home and tell my family. I ran for the bus, an open-backed double decker. I threw my sleeping bag in the luggage rack and headed upstairs. Then I heard someone shouting upstairs asking if anyone had a sleeping bag as one had rolled off the bus. I had to get off the bus at the Central Station. Then I ran all the way back up Northumberland Street asking passers-by if they had seen a sleeping bag until a person said yes and that it had been handed into a shop.

ncjMedia

Queuing in Saville Row for tickets for the Beatles, December 1964.

Was it all worth it? Well the concerts at the City Hall were brilliant with all of us screaming our heads off and the girls fainting with excitement. We didn't hear a word of the songs but the atmosphere was electrifying.

So who remembers sleeping out for the Stones? And does whoever handed my sleeping bag in remember? I never got a chance to thank them.

Margaret Dinsdale

ncjMedia

The Rolling Stones stirring up a storm at the City Hall 1 October, 1965.

When tickets for the Rolling Stones concert at the Odeon went on sale, my friend and I sneaked out of the house in the middle of the night to make our way into town to join the queue. We didn't have enough money for the all-night bus so set off to walk from Longbenton. We were stopped by the police on Matthew Bank and when they found out where we were going they decided to take us home, telling us all the time how smelly and scruffy the Stones were – which to two 15 year old girls only served to enhance their allure. Amazingly, they didn't see us into the house so as soon as they were gone we made our way back to town. Our parents were most surprised to see us on the next day's TV news practising our screaming for the television cameras outside the Odeon when we were supposed to have been tucked up in bed!

June Sains

Sleeping out for the Beatles, December 1964. In 1963 4000 queued for 48 hours for tickets for the City Hall and worried parents prompted the police to mount 'chastity patrols'.

Folk Clubs

When we weren't in the coffee bars we went to folk clubs. These were always in back rooms of pubs. I was too young to go to pubs but I had a deal with my parents. They trusted me to go as long as I promised not to drink alcohol.

Folk music was in its heyday. The Winning on Wallsend High Street, next to the grammar school, was our regular haunt. It was handy as we could walk home. It had its own regular performers plus visits from up-and-coming musicians like Boys of the Lough's, Dave Richardson.

We also went to the Bridge Hotel regularly. In the 60s there was a ceilidh in the upstairs room one Thursday and a singer/guitar session in the small basement room the next. These were run by Johnny Handle who usually played with the High Level Ranters. I can remember one night going up the stairs, saying to my friend 'but I'm not going to dance. I'll never get the steps right'. Unfortunately for me Johnny Handle had overheard and when he got up to introduce the first dance he looked around, as he always did, for a partner to help him to do the demonstration, saw me and dragged me up. I was very embarrassed at the time!

Don Partridge played at the Rex Hotel folk club down in Whitley Bay. He had his one man band machine with him. Rosie had been a big hit and he obviously made a bit of money because he was wearing a never-to-be forgotten snakeskin jacket.

Annie Moir

Geoff Laws

50

The Wesleyans

My first real link with the City Centre was with Brunswick Methodist Church where, in 1967, there was a coffee bar, at this time not quite the usual thing associated with the church. Once a month on a Saturday night a gospel group called The Wesleyans played pop songs but changed the lyrics to give a Christian message relevant to life in the 60s. It used to get packed out and some of us used to stand at the end of Brunswick Place on Fenwick's corner handing out leaflets in order to encourage more in.

Lynn Jacobs

The Wesleyans at Brunswick Church, 1967.

The Crestas and the Shades of Blue

I was mad about music, not just listening to it but playing it as well. I got my first guitar when I was 14 and at 16 was singing and playing in my first band, the Crestas. I lived with my parents near Stannington, but Newcastle was where everything was happening. We drove into the town in our old Bedford van at least twice a week after gigs or practice nights. It was before the breathaliser so God knows how we got back. We usually got home about 3 am; my folks must have been worried sick, but I didn't care then, I just wanted to be where it was happening. We used to go to the Club A 'Gogo (if you could prove you were 18 they stamped the back of your hand with an ultra violet circle to allow you into the Jazz Lounge). I saw some amazing bands in a very short space of time – Pink Floyd, Jimmy Hendrix, The Animals, Rod Stewart, Long John Baldry. I also went to the Quay Club near the Tyne Bridge. Another club on Pink Lane was more of a jazz place and was full of university hippies.

The Crestas were 'signed up' by Johnny Taw's dance band to do half-hour pop music sets for the young people at various ballroom dancing venues around the North East. One of these was the Old Assembly Rooms near the Central Station. These were very grand affairs and we enjoyed watching the toffs.

The Crestas split up, but I was soon asked to join the Shades of Blue. Two directors of the Bailey Organisation turned up at a charity ball at the Gosforth Park Hotel. That was the break we needed and we started working the Dolce Vita and the Cavendish in Newcastle and all the other Bailey Clubs down as far as Birmingham and Blackburn. Often when we finished around 2.00am we went to the 'Chicken and Chip' at the top of Pink Lane (there was another one in the Haymarket). All the groups used to meet there, and the roadside would be jammed with six-wheel-base transits with blacked out windows. If by some chance we couldn't get served we went to the British Rail canteen

Pink Lane, 1960s.

down a narrow walkway at the Central Station. If that failed it was Bowers, opposite the station. Bowers was awful – they used to cook your food on the metal plate that you ate off!

We eventually got a recording contract with Decca – our first 45 was *Back in Time* and because of the title Baileys did a huge promotion ending up with the band dressed in old fashioned paisley jackets driving through town in a horsedrawn landau, with posthorns playing. We arrived at the Turks Head Hotel in Grey Street where there was a reception in the Red Rover Bar.

Nick Thorburn

Youth club group

I bought my first record, *Pipeline* by The Chantays, in Disc in Gosforth for the princely sum of 6s 8d and from then on I was hooked. I joined St George's Youth Club in Jesmond, where music played all the time and where I met many people with varying musical tastes, blues, soul, rock, folk to name but a few. I joined three other lads to form a group called The Rigg, later changed to The Revolution. Our drummer, Dags, was a regular at the Club A 'Gogo and had great stories about The Animals, Spencer Davis Group, Junco Partners, Geno Washington and other famous musicians. I always regretted not getting to the A 'Gogo more – I usually went to gigs at The City Hall where I saw The Stones, The Byrds (my favourite group of all time) and many others. I remember the night when I went to see Moby Grape, it was during the days when you had five or six groups on twice a night and I was going to the second house. By this time the show was running late and when it got to about 9.30 the presenter came out and said there was only time for one more group. What was it to be? Family or Moby Grape? I couldn't believe all the fans voted for Family (who were on in Middlesbrough the next night) and Moby Grape disappeared to San Francisco without playing.

After Disc shut down I bought my records at Windows; most Saturdays found me there, usually in one of the cubicles listening to some new sounds. The place was packed in those days.

Mik Richardson

Mik Richardson

The Revolution pose on Osborne Road, near St George's church.

The Junco Partners

The 60s were a time when the brakes were let off musically. It was the perfect time to be a teenager and we weren't following the music of our parents. By 1959 it seemed that nearly every kid got a Spanish guitar for Christmas and was in a skiffle group.

By the early 60s those of us who had persevered with our guitars had formed groups at school and in youth clubs. We honed our skills playing complicated Shadows tunes as well as some Rock and Roll classics and copied all the songs on our Dansette Record Players. The

Everybody was in a band. A Newcastle skiffle group, 1960.

revolution came in 1962 when the Beatles and then the Stones burst on the scene. Suddenly there were hundreds of places to play, with teenage dances, social clubs and other clubs encouraging a younger audience.

In 1962, and under-age, I blagged my way into the Downbeat Club and saw a fantastic band which later became the Animals. Soon after I went to the Club A 'Gogo with fellow Junco-to-be Ronnie Barker and we saw Sonny Boy Williamson. For the first time I saw the power of R'n'B first hand.

The Juncos came together in late 1963 and in spring 1964 we auditioned at the Club A 'Gogo. Ronnie's school pal 'Top Mod' John Anderson was impressed enough to want to join and he suggested another mutual friend Charlie Harcourt from the very successful Berries to play lead guitar. We also enticed Pete Wallis, who played organ, away from another successful band.

The Club A 'Gogo manager allowed us to rehearse there, and we turned up one night in July 1964 to find a huge crowd invited for an Animals' homecoming party and were persuaded to play. It was only our second gig but we went down a storm. The Animals' manager offered us a gig at the Star Club Hamburg! In trepidation, we went home to tell our parents that we wanted to pack in our jobs. We were aged just between 17 and 19 and it would have been unthinkable five years earlier, but the 1960s changed the attitudes of everyone, and while our parents were concerned, they allowed us to turn professional – and it was as easy as that.

We immediately took over from the Animals at the Club A 'Gogo and Downbeat and, played frequently at the Mayfair and Majestic, and at Sunderland's Bay Hotel and Cubana and Blue Note Clubs. We ventured to Carlisle, Sheffield and all points between sometimes playing twice a day.

What was so great about the 1960s was the explosion in musical styles, by early 1965 we were playing complicated James Brown tunes and venturing into Soul music and by 1967 it was west coast rock, by 1968 Psychedelia and Flower Power and by 1969 progressive rock as well as our first love, R'n'B.

Six years on the national rock club and college circuit followed, playing with The Who, Rod Stewart, Jethro Tull, Jimi Hendrix, John Mayall Band, and many others. We toured as backing band to blues giants Howlin' Wolf and Freddie King in 1969 and were delighted to gain Wolf's respect.

The Juncos split in 1971 but re-formed in 1978 and returned to their R'n'B roots.

Dave Sproat, Junco Partners

Junco Partners

Cooler than cool, Junco Partners in their 1964 line-up. They took over from the Animals at the A 'Gogo in 1964 – their big break!

From The Aristokats to Lindisfarne

I would probably never have been involved with the music business if my Gran had not wanted me to be a priest. I passed the 11 Plus exam in 1959 and instead of enrolling at the local high school my parents got me a place at St Cuthbert's Catholic Grammar School in the West End of Newcastle. As I lived about ten miles away at the coast it meant a journey through the city every day for the next decade as I progressed through school, art college and my first, short-lived full time job.

I formed my first band in 1962 with Simon Cowe and we played together on-and-off for about 30 years. We were called the Aristokats and our first musical performances were confined to family gatherings, social clubs and intervals at the local Bingo Hall. At that time I could only dream about playing at a real gig in the city centre. By 1963-64 I was in the Druids and we began to travel further, but still hadn't made our debut in the city. By 1966 I had met Rod Clements and, inspired by Chicago Blues, the Beatles, Bob Dylan and Brown Ale, we began to assemble our perfect group. We were big fans of the Junco Partners, and used them as a template. I was regularly spending weekends in Newcastle, hanging around the music shops, Barratts on New Bridge Street, Maxie Share's in the Grainger Market and

Kitchen's in Ridley Place where our pal Mark saw his first ever Fender Strat (red of course). We bought most of our records at Windows in the Central Arcade or Jeavons in Percy Street. If I was hungry there was the Rumbling Tum or the Palletta; if I fancied a drink there was the Haymarket, the Blyth and Tyne or the Bridge Hotel. Teenage fashion was taking off in a big way but our taste in clothes mostly came from the Army Surplus store or

Ray Laidlaw

The Aristokats, around 1962, Ray Laidlaw on drums.

City Stylish, we weren't too bothered. Jeans were a different matter, they had to be the right brand and Marcus Price on Percy Street was the only place you could buy Levis.

We spent a lot of time watching other bands, either visiting big names or other local musicians, Alan Hull and Mickey Gallagher in the Chosen Few, Bryan Ferry in the Gas Board, Ray Jackson in the Autumn States. We knew most of them. We'd go to the Majestic or the Mayfair (crammed with 2000 people on a Tuesday for four local bands). The New Orleans Jazz Club was good for a bit of blues or the Quay Club opposite the Crown Posada where Geordie musicians would jam into the early hours. The best venue was the Club A 'Gogo on Percy Street. That was our spiritual home where we saw all of the big names. We were called Downtown Faction by then and got our first gig at the Gogo in September 1967. It felt like we'd just played Shea Stadium, what a buzz! A few months earlier we'd played at a gathering in the Handyside Arcade below the Gogo. It had been re-christened Arcadia and was full of hippy clothes and book shops. It was also home to Greg Burman's amplifier works and Joe Robertson's music management company. The youth had taken over.

For most of the 1960s I was still living with my parents so made many a late night journey down the Coast Road to Tynemouth. Sometimes in our battered group van, sometimes hitching and once or twice walking the whole way, thrilled by the music I'd just heard and making plans for the future.

There was incredible energy around during that period. and loads of co-operation between writers, actors, poets and musicians. We really felt that our time was coming and things were changing for the better. It certainly changed for us as Rod, Simon and I were joined by Ray Jackson and Alan Hull. As the sixties drew to a close we were performing together as Brethren. Six months later we became Lindisfarne.

Ray Laidlaw

Downtown Faction gig around 1966.

In 1969, free outdoor music events were a new and exciting development. Hyde Park, Golden Gate Park, why not Leazes Park? I telephoned the council and someone came to meet me in the park the next day. We looked around for a good site and he gave me permission there and then. I rounded up other bands and borrowed a flat back truck for a stage. On August Bank Holiday Monday 1969, Newcastle had its first free open-air rock gig. We parked up a couple of the group vans near the stage and put our PA speakers on the roofs. The nice man from the council arranged for an electrician to come over and supply power from a street lamp! Honest!

About 2000 people turned up and listened to some of Newcastle's best bands plus a folk group called the Callies and a local singer songwriter – Alan Hull was his name. Our band, Downtown Faction, went on last and we finished our set with an impromptu protest song, *Haircut Blues*. It was sung by our guitar player Simon Cowe who had just been given an ultimatum by his employer; lose the long hair or your job. Simon saw an opportunity for a bit of agitprop and berated his boss in song to a delighted audience as a hairdresser mate of ours chopped off his ginger tresses (see the colour section for a photo of this momentous event). We made all the local papers and everyone had a ball. No licence, no health and safety, no security, no problems.

Ray Laidlaw

Alan Hull in the park, 1969.

Lukie's youth club

My dad was the vicar at St Luke's (or Lukie's as it was known) Wallsend. In 1963-4, he replaced the AYPA (Anglican Young People's Association) with a youth club, which was held in the church hall.

Saturday night was dance night with a live band – Zulu, who quickly became the Autumn States. I don't know how my dad made the connection with them except that the lead singer Jacka (Ray Jackson) lived near by. Jacka later joined another well known band, Downtown Faction, before becoming a founder member of Lindisfarne. The Autumn States did cover versions of Rhythm and Blues and Motown – the most memorable for me were Bruce Channel's *Hey Baby*, the Drifters' *Saturday Night at the Movies* and the Stones' *Satisfaction* and *Get off of my Cloud*.

Sometimes the youth club had a folk night – Jacka was the first person I knew to play the mandolin and he came along one night and played the classic *Irene Goodnight* – very memorable.

Annie Moir

Ray laidlaw

| Representation | Open Door Management (0632) 27787 | Agency | Terry King Associates 25, Haymarket, LONDON S.W.1. Tel: 01–930–1771 |

The manager's tale

A clerk at the office I worked in asked if I'd manage his group, the Colts, so I set about getting them bookings. I took 10 per cent of the fee. Soon I had a number of groups to look after and found the secret was to tie up the venue and take pressure off the management. Mike Figgis, who played trumpet in the Colts, asked me to manage his other group, the Gas Board. They were about to lose their lead singer, Bryan Ferry, a talented art student at Newcastle University who eventually went on to found Roxy Music.

Sometimes we had a few problems. The Gas Board needed transport so I bought an old ambulance for them. I well remember the summons from Peterlee Magistrates' Court listing 32 defective offences … and another time the Colts' van was broken into and all the equipment stolen – they weren't insured! We got it all back though, after paying an 'informant'.

One morning I called round to collect a gig fee from the Gas Board's flat in Jesmond and was greeted by a scantily dressed young lad who said they were asleep. I didn't realise until years later that the sweet smell was cannabis – how naive!

Malcolm Dix

Dix Enterprises group, the Colts.

Bryan Ferry

The Gas Board, Bryan Ferry far right, Newcastle University, 1965-66. The Fine Art Department was a focus for 'cool'. Bryan, torn between painting and music, would go on to found the ultra-cool Roxy Music in London. Mike Figgis would become a successful film director.

I'd supported Newcastle United since I was 12 and when Joe Harvey joined the team in 1962 they really started to perform. I got friendly with the lads. The team was captained by Stan Anderson and they achieved promotion in 1965, the highlight being the 2-0 victory over Bolton Wanderers.

Because of disputes between the club and the City Council over redevelopment of the ground, St James' Park didn't meet the criteria to host World Cup matches so in 1966 the city was deprived – a great shame! But I was determined the city must have a role so the World Cup Ball was organised at the Mayfair. The Beatles didn't play at dances any more (I did contact Brian Epstein to ask!) but we went ahead with the Colts, Georgie Fame, Chris Farlowe and the Thunderbirds, Alan Price (though he got laryngitis and was replaced by Wayne Fontana and the Mindbenders) the Gas Board, and the Junco Partners. Quite a line-up!

We invited all the World Cup teams and Joe Harvey came with his players. We even used the pirate radio ship in the North Sea to advertise it and toured Newcastle in the group van with a loudspeaker. We sold out and even so there were queues round the block. That night there were more than 3,500 in the Mayfair, and Chris Farlowe's Out of Time was number one in the hit parade that day! What a success!

Malcolm Dix

Malcolm Dix

Psychedelic light shows

We organised many concerts with live bands at Rutherford College hall. As well as designing posters we decorated the hall with materials we managed to scrounge. Crepe paper seemed to figure quite a lot, often stretched from floor to ceiling. Psychedelic light shows were a big thing in clubs so we set up our own rudimentary version by fixing up a slide projector to a record turntable. Someone welded a strip of springy steel to the deck so that each time it revolved it clicked the button on the projector and changed the slide. We didn't study industrial design for nothing!

We were fortunate that some of the bands that played for us had their biggest hits between being booked and playing the gigs so we enjoyed the stars at a much reduced fee. Joe Cocker after *With A Little Help From My Friends*; Brian Auger and the gorgeous Julie Driscoll after *Wheels on Fire*; Fleetwood Mac after *Albatross*, to name but a few.

Geoff Laws

One of the biggest gigs was a concert at the City Hall as part of the Newcastle Students Arts Festival. We wanted a really original name and I came up with THE NON-VIOLENT SEXLESS FULLY CLOTHED SHOW. The line up of bands was quite something: Julie Driscoll with Brian Auger and The Trinity, Mason, Capaldi, Wood, Frog (later Traffic), Fairport Convention, and The John Hiseman Colosseum. There were poets, lights and films. One of the musicians remarked on seeing the title of the gig that it didn't sound like it was going to be much fun …

A mate and I painted a banner which stretched right across the City Hall stage with the name of the concert. I worked on it late into the night at the friend's flat then walked home with it in a holdall. It was about 2.00am and a police car drew up alongside me and inquired what I had in the bag. I said it was a banner and the cop immediately assumed that I was preparing to go on a protest march (quite common at the time). I explained that it was for the gig at the City Hall, told him the title and he went away.

Geoff Laws

Club A 'Gogo

'My baby found a new place to go
Hangs around town at the Club A 'Gogo.' (Club A 'Gogo, The Animals, 1964)

'The place is full of soul!' (Club A 'Gogo, the Animals, 1964)

Entrepreneur and music businessman Mike Jeffery founded several clubs in Newcastle in the early 1960s including the Downbeat, the Marimba, and most famously the A 'Gogo. The A 'Gogo, on Percy Street, consisted of two rooms above the canteen which served the bus station next door. It specialised in the blues. Mike Jeffery would go on to manage the Animals, who became the A 'Gogo's resident band in 1963 (Eric Burdon also provided the decor), and ultimately Jimi Hendrix. Mike Jeffery was killed in a plane crash in 1973.

Teenagers Bill Lancaster and his pal Tony ventured into Newcastle from Blaydon in the early 1960s, tempted by the Downbeat Club, excitement, girls, jazz. They explored Lindano's coffee bar at the bottom of Pink Lane, and La Pallette (the Palletta) on Blackett Street. Then, they found Club A 'Gogo.

Blackett Street was a good place for picking up local intelligence. Two young lads from Gosforth, similarly dressed, with whom we'd become pally in La Pallette, told us excitedly about their first visit to the Club A 'Gogo the previous evening. We joined them the following Friday. We met them at the Monument and within five minutes we were in the A 'Gogo entrance in Percy Street. A young man, who looked like a student, sat on a table a few yards inside the door, deeply preoccupied reading a paperback. He lifted his head, smiled at the four of us, took our money, one and sixpence, and gave us directions: up two flights of stairs, passing the busworkers' canteen on the way and into the Young Set. We were too young, he informed us, to enter the Jazz Lounge. The initial disappointment was quickly offset. We entered what seemed to me the darkest room I'd ever been in. But before I could adjust my eyes I was transfixed: *I'm Mad Again* by John Lee Hooker blasted out of the speakers and by the time Tony's face came into relief I could see that he was in heaven.

Hooker was followed by *Can't Sit Down* and this uptempo R & B number brought the crowd onto the dance floor. Many of the faces I recognised as co-habitees of my recently discovered daytime haunts. Most were under 20 and the atmosphere was electric. My sense of exuberant surprise was compounded when dancing commenced. There was no sign of ritualist jiving, with its self conscious, well practised choreography. Instead, male and female stood around in groups and started to shake. They never held hands, but I soon noticed that the 'Shake' or the 'Blues' as it was known locally, was in fact rather sophisticated. Hips and arms moved slightly, legs occasionally trembled, and shoulders swung laconically. The main characteristic of the dancers was their determination to be 'cool'. Not the self-centred coolness of the ted, who hardly glanced at his partner whilst he chewed gum and bopped the movements practised alone in his bedroom on countless evenings. No, this 'cool' was more subtle, the movements were both spontaneous and restrained, and driven by a new collective vibration.

We were soon at the A 'Gogo every Friday and Saturday night. The music and the clothes changed quickly. The diet of blues and R & B was joined by the outpourings from the Mersey, the Stones, Surf, and early soul. The 'look' that we had created in late 1962 from innovative sorties into ex-army stores soon gave way to a more commercialised uniform. Beatle jackets, polka dot shirts, Chelsea boots, leather waistcoats … Mod culture was emerging and a brief but wonderful period was rapidly over. There was

only one irritant to those halcyon months and that was my failure to get past Crombie into the Jazz Lounge …

Liz Nicholson

Bill Lancaster (extract from 'After Coffee at Sapparetti's', Northern Review, 1996.)

The good thing about the Gogo for the over 18s was that you paid one entrance fee, watched the band in the Young Set, then saw them all over again in the Jazz Lounge.

I was a bit young to see the Animals play at the Gogo but one band I did see there for the first time was the supergroup Cream. I found out about Cream's appearance by word of mouth before they had even released their debut album 'Fresh Cream' in 1966. I expected to be one of a small band of

Dick Heckstall-Smith on sax at the A 'Gogo 1968.

keen Eric Clapton fans with the place to ourselves, however when I arrived the queue was right along Percy Street.

We watched them in the Young Set then followed them as they walked through the crowd to the Jazz Lounge, carrying their guitars. The stage in the Lounge was only a couple of feet high, the amplifiers were piled up on the sides and speakers were stuck up on a slender wooden frame which was meant to be a decorative feature suspended above the stage.

We stood right up to the stage while people piled in behind and the crowd pressed so tight you couldn't have fallen down even if you fainted. There we stood for what seemed like hours while the band relaxed in the dressing room. Then eventually they appeared again and we enjoyed a couple of hours of painfully loud music. Amplification was less sophisticated then. Our ears used to ring for days afterwards.

I can still picture Ginger thrashing away at his drums and between songs drinking from a milk bottle which he kept next to him on the floor. The bottle contained a clear liquid which I suspect wasn't water.

Geoff Laws

Liz Nicholson

Above, Julie Driscoll, *below,* Mick Taylor. *Both at the A 'Gogo, 1968.*

Liz Nicholson

Club A'Gogo
HOME OF THE ANIMALS.

Tonite
8—2   Another Ravin' Young Set
5/-   Weekend   7.30–11.
              From   3/-
            Ricky Tic Windsor
          R. and B. Showband
HOGSNORT RUPERT
        & HIS GOOD, GOOD, BAND
              From Leeds
THE DAWNBREAKERS
Sat
8—2   From Manchester Young Set
8/6   Exciting New
              Group   7.30–12.
ST. LOUIS UNION   4/-
              +
HOGSNORT RUPERT
Licensed till 2 a.m.
Blackjack. Steakroom Roulette and
              till 2 a.m.
Saturday, March 20th—from U.S.A.
              T-BONE WALKER

J.G. Windows,
Central Arcade, 1966,
first port of call for
records.

Does anyone
remember Hogsnort
Rupert?

BRIGHT LIGHTS BIG CITY

The Maj

I heard it said almost every day, especially in my teens. From my mum, aunty or gran – 'I'm going shopping over the town'; and from mates – 'We're gannin ower the Toon' – the ower bit meaning crossing the Tyne Bridge and, of course, the town was Newcastle. Despite being a Gateshead lad, I remember spending a great deal of the sixties in the 'toon'.

Friday night was my Majestic night – being an apprentice, I could only afford one night on the town. It was quickly home from work, hand over the board money and into the bath, on with the Marcus Price suit and it would be the only time during the week you would wear a tie. Jeans were banned from the Majestic too. Timing was down to the second. Just as you were ready, the knock came at the back door, the lads were waiting – all in Marcus Price suits – and then down to the bus stop. (Taxis? Give me a break!)

First stop for a 16-year-old was The Waterloo on Bath Lane, close to the Majestic, and three pints of Scotch. I may have been only 16, but I knew my limit. The oldest of the lads would be 17 but we all prided ourselves as easily passing for 18, well at least we thought we were getting away with it. You watched for that tell-tale sign of the top of a copper's helmet passing down the side of the pub, sticking above the frosty window. Your heart missed a beat in case he peeked through the door, your confidence suddenly taking a dive. Then, again, it was all clear. Now all there was to do was to finish your three drinks and game of darts and head for 'the Maj'.

We had worked it out. 8.30pm was the best time to get there – but there was a final hurdle. After paying, if you didn't cross the foyer in a straight line (the effects of alcohol) the bouncer would have you out the door, and there was always one of us a bit dodgy. We'd hustle him by and into they dance hall. Walking into the Maj ballroom was stepping into a magical world. The music, the atmosphere, the girls. You split into twos, walked the floor, enjoyed the girls, the swinging skirts, the tight skirts. They gave you a smile, your mate agreed, and

The Majestic, 1959.

onto the floor you stepped. To get the girl you wanted you had to be a step in front of your pal, but the girls' smiles drew you in. You might only have danced a few seconds before the music stopped and you introduced yourselves, asked where they lived and it was off again, bopping, twisting, even the Locomotion, whatever, the night was young.

After the usual *Save The Last Dance For Me*, it was time to go for the girls' coats and a meeting outside. If you had scored you got to walk your girl home, if you were flush it might have been a late bus ride, but it didn't really matter. The end to a perfect night.

ncjMedia

A lunchtime session at the Maj, 1962.

Yes, you had to be careful, there were certain areas where it was dangerous, even in those days. Gangs were more prevalent then, and they had their areas – it might not have been exactly West Side Story, but you had to keep one eye on what was happening. One big difference about Newcastle in those days, the police all seemed about two ft taller than today, in reality many could have been a foot taller. And they were constantly watching, they didn't spend their time talking to each other, they never missed a thing.

But there was one night at the Majestic that was really special. No, it wasn't a girl. A fortnight earlier I had noticed a small pile of flyers on a little table in the foyer. Checking them out, I saw they were for a band that I'd just heard on the radio – The Beatles. Tickets were about six bob I

The Majestic Ballroom, Westgate Road and Clayton Street, 1966.

think, a lot of money, but they did sound special. A fortnight later I remember walking up to the Star pub, opposite the Majestic and there was a crowd of girls under the back-stage room window, stopping the traffic and, hanging out of the window was John Lennon, shouting down at them. Inside we went and you could feel the excitement building. Soon the four mopheads came on, and within seconds everyone had stopped dancing and closed in on the stage.

I was quite tall and happy to be at the back – but a girl beside me was upset, she couldn't get through the melee, couldn't see the Fab Four, so there was only one thing a gentleman could do – she draped her legs over my shoulders and I gave her the best seat in the house – no complaints from me. It was a great night, the atmosphere was unbelievable and The Beatles, playing live, were everything I hoped they'd be.

Ray Marshall

Sometimes on nights off we went to the Maj. There were always loads of girls there, and for some peculiar reason they all walked anti-clockwise round the dance floor. Nobody has ever explained to me how that started.

Nick Thorburn

The Oxford

On a Monday and Thursday night, Eileen and I would go on our regular jaunt to the Oxford Galleries, it cost 3s 9d to get in and we used to dance our little feet off to Tamla Motown songs as they were always our favourite. Every time I hear *Build me up Buttercup*, I think of those times. We had our own special steps to I *Heard it through the Grapevine*.

Karin Musson

OXFORD GALLERIES

COME DANCING THIS WHIT WEEKEND to
DON SMITH and his ORCHESTRA
Friday 8.0—1.0 ... Admission 7/-
Saturday 7.30—11.30 Admission 7/-
SAT. TEA DANCE 3.0—5.30, Ad. 2/9
Whit Monday off the Record Top of
The Pops, 12—5. Admission 2/6.
And 7—11. Admission 3/-.
Junior Disc Session, Saturday morn-
ing, 11—1 p.m. Admission 1/-.

Thursdays was for the 14 to 17 year olds as there was no alcohol on sale. This wasn't a problem though as the Portland pub opposite turned a blind eye to under age drinkers, though not as much as the Bacchus on Newgate Street opposite the Co-op.

Joe Rogerson

They had a great band and two great singers, Kay could imitate anyone, especially Dusty Springfield, and Terry was very good too. Friday night was the night to meet the lads and Sunday night was for the serious dancers – all the usual ballroom plus Latin American and rock 'n roll.

Brenda Woods

I think I was about 13 or 14 when the Oxford Rooms opened for two hours on a Saturday morning for teenagers. They played the latest hit tunes – The Animals' *House of the Rising Sun* was my favourite as it went on for ages. You danced in a circle with your friends and put your handbags in the middle so you could keep an eye on them. One soft drink lasted you the whole morning.

Linda Gray

You danced what was called 'the Oxford Shuffle', as there were so many people on the dance floor, you couldn't stride out very much. But it was ideal if you danced with a girl you liked as you were squashed together on the floor. When it was your birthday you received a cake and a bottle of wine. Don Smith was the band leader in those days.

J.J. Connell

The boys walked around the place anti-clockwise and the girls clockwise, this meant you did not miss any opportunities to meet the opposite sex. There was no alcohol sold in the Oxford on these nights so we would sneak a couple of pints in the Lord Nelson or the Trafalgar, they weren't too fussy if you were under age. But you couldn't get a pint in the Portland.

Tony Groves

The Oxford, 1971.

The Mayfair

When we booked them in early 1966 nobody much knew them But when they came to Newcastle that night in July to perform at our school dance, they'd been in the charts with *Hold Tight* and *Hideaway*.

What brave, intrepid convent school girls we were. Aged 17 we organised the biggest dance hall in the city – The Mayfair – filled it to capacity with world cup footballers, including the Chilean team, with 'stuck in the 50s' teachers to chaperone us young, fabulous teenagers, and of course Dave Dee, Dozy, Beaky, Mick and Tich. What a night – back stage virgin groupies, the place jumping and alive with happy, free spirited friends! We had pulled it off through sheer ignorance and enthusiasm.

Dave Dee, Dozy, Beaky, Mick & Tich

THE SECT & THE PIECES OF FIVE

with

at

MAYFAIR BALLROOM

on

WEDNESDAY, 20th JULY, 1966

8 p.m. – 1 a.m.

Late Transport

Tickets 7/6

Bar until 12 midnight

Sheila Harrison (nee O'Reilly) and Jennifer Swaddle

We used to go to the Mayfair; they gave you chicken and chips in a basket with your entrance ticket. The band leader there was Mr Bench.

J.J. Connell

Likely lads

In the early days we were all Mods, buying our clothes from City Stylish or Marcus Price using Provi tickets. Most of us had accounts at John Temple the Tailors where we used to have our suits made with jackets at thumb length, flaps on the pockets and 15-inch centre vents.

We used to go to the Oxford on a Thursday night dressed to kill with our Levi's Sta-Prest trousers and our stripy Ben Sherman shirts with button-down collars. Another place was the Club A 'Gogo. We were too young to get into the Jazz Lounge for a drink. Still, there was always the Lion and the Lamb, The Bacchus or The Old George in the Bigg Market.

After the Gogo we would spend the rest of the night at Bowers all-night café opposite the Central Station and get the first train home. We used to tell our mothers that we stayed at each other's houses, which was fine until the mothers met!

Fashions changed, hair grew a lot longer and now we were Hairies. Huge mobs of young men knocked about the town together, gathering at The Blackett (Simpsons) and The Café Royale opposite. We also used to go to The Man in the Moon, The Pineapple, The Lowther or Carter's Wine Lodge to sample the Merrydown cider. The bar staff rationed us to two drinks each because of its strength.

Opposite the Pineapple was a shop called Sacha and my brother and I used to buy our boots there because they sold sizes up to a nine. Men's shops didn't cater for men wearing women's boots. Due to our appearance we couldn't get into our old haunt, the Oxford, but they weren't so strict at the Dolci as long as you had a tie on. Most weeks there were top bands on at the Mayfair and it was a very popular place for young people, it is a sacrilege that it ended up a car park under the Gate.

On a Saturday afternoon the Mods used to gather under the 'Dirty Angel' (or the 'mucky angel') as it was called, in the Haymarket.

Tony Groves

Young and in love

I met my husband, Alan, in September 1961 at the Newbiggin Dance Studios on New Bridge Street, when I was 16 years old and he was 21. We didn't go to the dance classes, only the 'social' afterwards, much to the disgust of the dancing instructors! Our first official date was to see *Whistle Down the Wind* at Blacks Regal picture house on Shields Road, Newcastle. We didn't have telephones so dates had to made in advance and you hoped your date would turn up as promised. If they didn't you knew you were 'chucked'! I usually met Alan at Cook's Corner in town. Our favourite places were the Oxford Galleries, the Downbeat Club and the Majestic where we saw Gene Vincent and many other popular groups. We saw Jerry Lee Lewis at the City Hall and the fabulous Matt Monroe at the Dolce Vita. We danced and sang to the Beatles, Ray Charles and many others.

Beryl Turner

Beryl Turner

Opposite, New Bridge Street, 1964. The Oxford is top right.

Hanging out with the Beats and the Mods

Our night-time haunts were the Downbeat, especially for the all-nighter on Saturdays (your mother didn't know about that one!) and the Maj on Westgate Road. Oh, how I remember crying on the front steps when Manfred Mann cancelled their gig at the last minute. We did get to meet the Kinks when they played there though. We would go to the Mayfair occasionally to see bands like the Pretty Things – I have fond memories of hanging onto the revolving stage kissing Phil May's foot – it seemed like a good idea a the time. There was an occasional visit to the Gogo (you had to 'dress up' to get in – no beats allowed) when there was a good band playing. Favourites were Long John Baldry's Steam Packet, Wilson Pickett, Bo Diddley, Jimi Hendrix and of course the Animals.

Wrong image

WHY is it that very often we in the north are considered to be uncouth, and yet almost all the trouble in the "Mods" v. "Rockers" battle occurs in the south of England? — S. NICHOLS, Cranwell Drive, Woodlands Park Estate, Wideopen.

Letter, Evening Chronicle, 1965.

June Sains

The Downbeat – I used to be a beatnick then. I wore a duffle coat (with a ban the bomb badge) black stockings and a long black jumper as well as white lipstick and black eye make-up.

The Quay Club – I think it was best place ever. It was dark and dingy with loud Tamla Motown Music playing – it always smelt damp and we always had to queue up for along time to get in.

The New Orleans Jazz Club – The club was always full. We only went for the lads!!

The Oxford – I always seemed to get drunk on Pernod and Lime when I went there. The best night was a Monday but unfortunately there was work on a Tuesday and that took the shine off a bit.

Lynda Mason

The Muscle Inn was at the bottom of Dean Street, under the Railway Line. In the very early days it was the coolest joint. You went up loads of narrow stairs to a room used by body builders through the day. On a Friday and Saturday night it was a beat club that could hold around 80 people. It was characterised by loads of fights, long hair, combat jackets and loud music. The Rolling Stones played there regularly.

Malcolm Henderson

La Dolce Vita

Dakota Staton at the Dolce Vita, around 1968.
'There was lots of gambling at the Dolce Vita. And we saw
lots of acts like Dave Berry and Engelbert Humperdinck, when
he was Gerry
Dorsey. He was gor-
geous. Marvellous
cabarets.'
(Pauline Luke)

La Dolce Vita
Apply for Membership, 36-42, Low Friar St., Newcastle. Tel. 26793.
Proudly present all this week (Doors open 8) Cabaret 11 p.m.
The Fabulous KATHY KIRBY
Sensational Comedians DES & DAVE. Also the 3 ARCHDALE SISTERS
CASINO OPEN NIGHTLY at 9.30
Admission: Mon. to Fri. 10/-: | Sat. only 15/-—Come Early
Roulette : Dice : Chemin de | CASINO open every Sunday
Fer : Blackjack in Fabulous | at 9.30. Entrance, Coffee and
Casino | Snacks. All Free!

La Dolce Vita TELEPHONE 26793
PROUDLY PRESENT THIS WEEK
NEWCASTLE'S FIRST £3,000 CABARET
Tonight CABARET at 10.45 Open at 8 p.m.
From America especially for La Dolce Vita
THE FABULOUS MR. 'B'
BILLY ECKSTINE
Also RAFAEL DE SEVILLA AND HIS BALLET ESPANOL
All next week
JOE BROWN & HIS BRUVVERS
Also ETHNA CAMPBELL
APPLY FOR MEMBERSHIP NOW
DANCING TO THE BOB STEPHENSON SEXTET
CHEMIN-DE-FER, BLACKJACK AND ROULETTE NIGHTLY
Patrons please note—all Table Reservations to be taken up by
10 p.m. Monday to Friday, 9.30 Saturdays

Pubs in the 1960s.

Clockwise from above: Robinson's Wine Cellar, and the Nag's Head (Cloth Market); the Trafalgar, New Bridge Street; the Bacchus, Newgate Street. Opposite page, the Northumberland Arms, Northumberland Street.

Pubs and clubs

The first pub I tried was the Blackie Boy. I was 15. My friend and I went in about ten to three on a Saturday afternoon and had a bottle of Brown Ale each. By three o'clock we were the only ones left in the pub. The barman remarked, 'pass me those empty glasses and I'll buy you a pint when you are 18'. I couldn't get out of there quick enough!

Later we would always meet at the Northumberland Arms. This was a dirty old place but it seemed to end up as the start off point for a pub crawl. On the night Callers burnt down everyone was watching from the pub. We went through a stage of drinking 'Snake Bites' which in The Northumberland Arms consisted of cider and Newcastle Exhibition – you ordered one at the start of the night and left it a while until the sediment at the bottom of the glass was good and thick. We had singing competitions against lads from the West End, getting fairly loud as the night wore on.

Next stop usually was the Monkey Bar (the Market Lane) opposite the Fire Station. The main attraction was the jukebox. From there we would move on to The Rose and Crown and The Lowther roughly opposite each other.

At the Blackett Arms I saw the worst pub fight ever with about two dozen people fighting and throwing glasses at each other, people diving under tables to get away from it, me included. In this category too was the Golden Tiger in the Bigg Market, home of Viv a well known gay bloke, but as hard as nails, who played the part but was always good for a laugh. I can recall a coin which was glued to the floor so that when you bent down to pick it up Viv could check you out, as it were.

We also went to The Chain Locker, downstairs at the back of The Turks Head Hotel, the in place to go at one time. Other pubs to remember are The Haymarket Hotel, The Hotspur and The Strawberry, which was very popular on match days. There were literally hundreds of pubs, nearly all of them full.

Mik Richardson

BALMBRA'S
Olde Tyme Music Hall
7.45 TWICE NIGHTLY 9.15
Change of Programme Weekly
Fully Licensed : Phone 20015

*More pubs. Clockwise from
above: Balmbra's, Cloth Market;
The Turk's Head, Grey Street;
Café Royale, Nelson Street.*

Near the top of Grey Street was the Grapes pub, then a men-only bar. At the bottom of Grainger Street was the Douglas Hotel with its magnificent panelled buffet, resplendent with large oil paintings of Scottish Highland scenery – another men-only bar. Another pub of blessed memory was in High Friar Lane, along from the YMCA building (close to Grey's monument) known as Curley's (its proper name may have been the White Flag). The YM and Curley's bit the dust so that Eldon Square could rise up in their place.

In the Cloth Market two popular drinking places were Robinson's Wine Cellar with sawdust on the floor and large sherry casks that served as tables. Further down was the celebrated Balmbra's with regular Old Time Music Hall, where you sat at tables drinking and singing along to Geordie songs.

David Hughes

We met the Beatles in 1965. We were in the Turks Head, in the foyer with the revolving door, just deciding where to go next – would we go to the 69 Club? A guy came in, who turned out to be Justin Hayward from the Moody Blues and said 'Hello girls, where are you going?' And he sat down. And then he said 'Do you want to meet the Beatles?' And through the back we went. There were lots of roadies, and we couldn't ask for autographs, and sure enough there they all were! Ringo had a tassled jacket on. We were all smoking and chatting. There was a few of us sat on a settee and it went over … legs in the air! I had on a floral dress and a fox fur – it must have been my mother's!

Pauline Luke

If I Were a Rich Man

We lived in the back streets of Benwell and my father made a poor sort of living as a commercial traveller, selling door to door. He spent most of his nights as entertainment secretary for the RAFA club. The sixties changed that. My father had always hankered after a bit of fame and the high life. Then he met Mr Joe Lisle, a Newcastle businessman and became a follower of his.

Joe was in the entertainment business and, at the beginning of the sixties, Dad became his manager at the Gem Bingo club at the Big Lamp, and then The Borough at Wallsend. By 1963 he was in his element as the general manager of the 69 Club on Westgate Road, the Karlsen Club in North Shields and, by the end of the sixties, a director of the Tatler Club on Northumberland Street.

My mother became one of his croupiers and the two of them worked until two or three in the morning then, and after a night of drinking and socialising, they came home in his flash new Rover car.

My mother bought cocktail dresses and very high heeled shoes and used to tell us about the people who used to bet £5 at a time on a roll of the wheel. At the end of the night her box was stuffed with notes but she wasn't allowed to count them – she suspected that a cut was taken from them before the accounts were done. My dad used to boast about the famous people that he met, including Cliff Richard and the Kray Twins, and he just loved to splash his money around and play the big guy.

Although there was a lot more money about than there ever had been, it was rapidly being spent on the trappings of a new life style. My mother was keen to buy a new house, something she could never have imagined before, but she had to be content with a new council house as my father was not the savings type. We had been on the housing list for years with six of us in an upstairs flat but now, with only one child still at home, they got a house with a garden in a new development. I suspect my father had got to know someone in the council who had 'put in a good word'. My mother bought all new furniture and made her first garden – another dream come true. They had a fancy dress New Year's Eve party the first year they were there and later another big 'do' for his fiftieth birthday.

I think the sixties were the start of Newcastle becoming the Party City of the North and my father helped to pioneer it.

Norma Scott

In 1967 *North East Nightlife* magazine listed 11 night clubs in Newcastle: The Cavendish, La Dolce Vita, Club 69, The Emerson, Billy Botto's Club, Flamingo Club, Greys Club (with cellar Discotheque), Michael's, Piccadilly Club, Tatler Club, and the Birdcage Club. There were plenty of clubs to choose from. The Cavendish and La Dolce Vita belonged to Bailey's.

The YMCA

The YMCA was well past its best but the big, curved windows on the first floor overlooking Grey's Monument had probably the best viewpoint in Newcastle. They were filled by two huge leather settees which were worn and tattered. The room was like an Edwardian gentleman's club that had seen better days. We sat there for hours after work and on Saturday solving the problems of the world. The toasted tea cakes were a famous legend of the YMCA. They were toasted on an ancient grill behind a serving hatch and served with milky coffee from antique silver pots. The two staff seemed to be equally ancient.

At the other end of the building was a big noisy room where the young people hung out and listened to the latest pop music on a juke box. On the second floor was the restaurant which was another faded throwback to Edwardian times. Formal silver service and waitresses in proper serving attire was the norm. The food was very plain, English 'meat and two veg' but cheaper than most restaurants.

The YMCA, 1966.

Way up ever narrower stairs was the gym where the badminton club met and where I first met my wife to be. It had a big raftered and glass roof and the shuttle cocks sometimes got stuck up there.

David Rochester

The Morden Tower

In 1968 an art student took me to the Morden Tower to hear poet Adrian Mitchell. The Tower was really exciting, full of cool people who all seemed to know each other. We climbed the stone stairs from Back Stowell Street into the tiny room at the top. Everyone sat on the floor, or on the ledge around the wall. It was dark, damp, uncomfortable, wonderful. Tom and Connie Pickard ran the Tower, and Tom also ran the Ultima Thule bookshop in Handyside Arcade.

Anna Flowers

Tom Pickard at Morden Tower, 1964. Right, American beat poet Allen Ginsberg reads at the Tower in 1965.

Kindly loaned by Harmony Hall

Facing our store (Harmony Hall, on Newgate Street) was the Empire Theatre, and it was my task on Monday mornings to go backstage to find out if the visiting acts required any stage furnishings for their weekly show. In the early sixties we loaned a couple of high stools to the Everly Brothers and quite a few easy chairs for the artistes' dressing rooms.

One Monday morning Bruce Forsyth was rehearsing a dance routine while a stage cleaner with her heavy broom was sweeping only a few feet away; there was dust flying all over the place!

I enjoyed Eddie Cochrane and Gene Vincent during their week's stay. But the very best star was Shirley Bassey. She was here for six nights, performing twice nightly. On the first performance on the Monday night no more than 100 people were in the theatre but as the days passed the theatre was packed out. In the first show of the week you could hear the rustle of crisp packets and sweet papers from the older people in the front stalls as Shirley was singing.

Our store's payment for the occasional loan of furnishings was a very small advert on the stage fire curtain along with adverts for a few other local retailers. Our advert read 'Stage Furnishings Kindly Loaned By Harmony Hall Facing This Theatre'

Unfortunately the Empire closed down in 1963 and was demolished two years later to make way for the Newgate shopping centre and the Swallow Hotel.

Malcolm Cummings

The Empire Theatre, Newgate Street, 1963.

ESPRESSO BONGO

Coffee bars figured large in my life as a young teenager in Newcastle. There were several that we frequented but I'm not sure if we visited them all in rotation or if one came into fashion as another went out. The Tyneside Coffee rooms were a constant. I always think of them as deep red velvet and gold. We also went to the Rumbling Tum in Ridley Place, The Milkmaid on New Bridge Street (opposite the steps to the Central Library) and Mark Toney's on Grainger Street. These were early evening haunts.

Annie Moir

The Palletta

A favourite meeting place was a coffee bar called the Palletta. At least I think that was its name – we always called it 'The Pit' as it was in a basement. It was opposite the Blackett Street entrance to Fenwick's. We would listen to the latest records (on a juke box I presume) while we tried to make a cup of coffee last all afternoon.

If someone had money to buy a record (45rpm singles) we might all go to Windows and listen to it (perhaps another record too) in one of the booths before the purchase was made. It felt as though you were getting something for nothing if you had a free hearing before you bought the record.

Afterwards we might go to the Club A 'Gogo where Saturday afternoon was for the younger teenagers. We could dance round our handbags in the time honoured fashion to the latest Tamla Motown records and drink Hubbly Bubbly from the bottle through a straw.

On other occasions we would go to the Northumberland Road Baths – but only to the 'Ladies Plunge' which we favoured because it was quieter – at least until we arrived. Afterwards it was the Rumbling Tum, in Ridley Place, to drink coke and eat crisps or a Mars bar.

Jane Boyd (née Turnbull)

La Pallette, in a large cellar … this was the hangout of the toggle and corduroy brigade … the ex-army store facing La Pallette provided camouflage jackets, much in vogue with local beatnicks, and Lybro jeans, cut in the wide American style.

Bill Lancaster

Ridley Pace, 1966. The Rumbling Tum is on the left, about halfway down.

We went to the Palletta from about 1960. You could sit for hours in booths and watch who came downstairs. Eric Burdon used to come in a lot and say silly things. He was wild. He bounced in! The Marimba was a coffee bar on High Bridge, and there was a cellar downstairs. You had to have a meal to stay late, it was maybe three shillings, because otherwise you couldn't have live music.

Pauline Luke

As 'beats' our favourite hangouts were the Central Station, Eldon Square, and the Pit (Palletta) on Blackett Street, where the sympathetic waitresses would let you sit over one coke for several hours. There was also a tobacconist on Blackett Street where you could purchase cigarettes singly, 6d for a 'Passing Cloud' but they were only for special occasions as one could last most of the day!

June Sains

In 1968 I opened Le Sandwich Boutique in Shakespeare Street, the first of its kind in the town. We served Danish open sandwiches. Much to the annoyance of the police, we placed chairs and tables on the pavement which they regularly tried to make us remove – it is now, of course, common practice to do this.

Joseph Fisher

After Breakfast (With Peter) Costing 5/6d

Not exactly a coffee bar, the Cloth Market Café (right) inspired Newcastle poet Barry MacSweeney to write:

a girl in a hooped miniskirt leans against the white door
of the CLOTH MARKET CAFE
its 10.30 a.m. here are cabbages jewish
artichokes granny pippins & button mushrooms

(From 'After Breakfast (With Peter) Costing 5/6d' in *The Boy From the Green Cabaret Tells of his Mother*, Hutchinson, 1967).

Blackett Street, 1966. The trolley bus wires that criss-cross the air would soon be taken away. The YMCA is on the left, with the doorway to the below-ground Palletta coffee bar. Cars, of course, park where they like.

Left, Fenwick fashions around 1968.

Below, flower power fashions – local group the Gas Board (after Bryan Ferry's departure), gorgeous in flowered shirts and beads around 1967.

Opposite, a Barbara Hulanicki coat bought from the Biba mail order catalogue, winter 1969 (it cost £13 13s).

DEDICATED FOLLOWER OF FASHION

Marcus Price – the coolest shops in town

My father opened the first Marcus Price shop in Blyth in 1929. In around 1950 he managed to get a shop in Percy Street, Newcastle and that was the start of something a bit special. The 1950s was a very curious time. There were only three or four articles that seemed to sell: black trousers with turn ups, black and white salt-and-pepper tweed jackets, a few pullovers and an amazing range of shirts and ties. The window display probably featured 60 different shirts – every one boarded with stiff card pinned tightly. The ties were natty slim jims.

I remember the end of the flat cap. The guy that was selling them came into the Percy Street shop one day and my dad said, 'No, we're not taking any more,' pointing to piles of caps in the shop that just weren't selling, then he took the guy out into Percy Street. Dad asked him how many people were wearing caps – that's the acid test. There was no-one, yet 10 years earlier everyone wore a cap.

The 1960s arrived with a burst of energy and youth. I don't think any fashions since the 1960s caused so much of a culture shock. I suppose it reflected all the things that were going on in the world; political changes like the Civil Rights movement in the USA; a new sense of freedom; the fact that you didn't have to live with your parents and you had a bit more disposable income.

By 1960 I was running the Percy Street shop. We also had another shop in the Groat Market. It attracted more customers coming from places like Sunderland, Middlesbrough and Gateshead because their buses came into Worswick Street bus station and it was easier to reach from there. We were next to George Rye's shoe shop.

Dylan bought a jacket and a tie in the Groat Market shop. I was working in Percy Street and the phone rang. 'Dylan's in!' That was in 1965. We were popular with other musicians too. Lulu used to come in and buy clothes for her band, The Lovers. She'd say 'he'll have that, that and that.' She obviously knew the look she wanted. The singer Billy Eckstine ordered two pairs of pants made to measure and we sent them to him in Hollywood Boulevard! The band leader at the Oxford would pick three ties and buy a dozen of each of them – whether they were for the band I don't know.

I was a jazz person – jazz was massive, but there

Marcus Price

Percy Street, 1972. Marcus Price is just beyond Jeavons music shop. The entrance to the Club A 'Gogo, which was on the top floor of Handyside Arcade, is far right, though by 1972 the A 'Gogo had ceased to be.

was a lot of blues around too. Every big name seemed to come to Newcastle. I knew Alan Price well. One or two of us used to meet on Saturday lunchtimes in Pumphrey's. There was Alan Price, Nigel Stanger and John Walters who played with Alan Price (and later became a BBC producer – he produced John Peel).

We didn't cater for rockers, we dressed the mods. Jackson the Tailor was the place rockers went. Still, we did an awful lot of tailoring. Newcastle United footballers were a big part of trade. Our regulars included Frank Clark and Bryan 'Pop' Robson. We made Frank Clark's wedding suit.

As a shop we tried to be different – we didn't want anyone else in Newcastle to have the same lines. One of our best-sellers in the 1960s was the Ben Sherman shirt. The details like the pearl buttons and the hanging loop at the back were just right. We bought (and sold) so many that we were able to tell the manufacturer that we didn't want anyone else in Newcastle to sell them. Ben Sherman did a long version of the shirt which was a woman's knee-length frock. I remember a big rack in all the colours in the Percy Street Shop.

Another popular line in the 1960s was Levi jeans. Farnons was the only other shop in Newcastle to stock them. The Blyth shop stocked Levi's because they were a work jean and it was a working port – seamen could get them in New York and they wanted to get them in Blyth too. It was an industrial look. That was probably why we started stocking them in the Newcastle branches. Apparently the seamen used to hang them over the back of the ship and that bleached the colour and smoothed the fabric. Later the idea was taken up commercially and became known as salt washing. The problem with Levi's was that you couldn't get them all the time. The company claimed that the factories were supplying the US army in Vietnam and that was what caused the shortages.

Our typical customer was certainly young. We were never the cheapest clothes shop, but a lot of our customers were at art school. We were selling shirts at 21 shillings but the main shirt lines cost 27s 6d and some shirts sold for 32s 6d – that was a lot of money in the days when a girl working in C & A would earn £3 a week. I think things lasted a bit longer – fashions didn't change quite as quickly as they do now. Having said that, the Beatles jacket came and went fairly quickly. We did one in foam-backed fabric as well as one in leather. In the early 60s the price of a suit was £14, but then we imported an Italian suit with lined trousers that retailed at £27 10s. It was a huge price but we sold it. Then we saw the opportunity to move up-market was there and we started to import more stock. We would buy clothes from Holland and fly them into Newcastle but the paperwork was incredible.

We opened the Grey Street shop in 1967 as part of our move up-market. We were selling expensive articles from the beginning and stocked hand-made clothing and silks. When the average shirt cost between £1 10s and £2, the silk shirts in the Grey Street branch cost between £4 and £5. Normal ties cost between 8 and 10 shillings, but we charged 30 shillings for the pure silk ties in Grey Street. In fact the pure silk ties sold amazingly well and the manufacturers were astonished.

Other good sellers in the 1960s were three-buttoned, straight-fitting dark jackets with narrow lapels and muted stripes, Beatle-style collarless suits, flower power shirts and ties to match. We also sold those awful smelly afghans and leather vests. We were good on coats and raincoats. One of lecturers in the University fine art department had a wife who made flowered ties. We bought them and they sold well. I went to Liberty's in London and bought yards and yards of their fabric. I had it made up into ties and we sold thousands. A lot of 1960s fashion was very dandyish, and of course anyone could wear a flowered tie to show how free and trendy they were.

Marcus Price

Marcus Price

The Percy Street shop with Marcus Price assistant, Ray Simpson, one of the sharpest dressers in town, behind the counter.

Marcus Price, Groat Market – when Dylan came to shop

I managed Marcus Price's shop in the Groat Market all through the 1960s. You went past Pudding Chare and it was next to George Rye's shoe shop. It had a central entrance and a long window on each side of the door. Shirts were a big thing then. People always wanted shirts and ties. It was great fun!

We stocked ties in stripes and polka dots. Later, when flower power came, all the ties had to be in flowery material. We were going out and buying curtain material and remnants and so on and sending them away to our tie manufacturers. They were a load of rubbish! They wouldn't hang right. We sold flowery shirts too and then the more pretentious manufacturers used to do them in boxes with matching ties … hideous. And then there were the hipster trousers made up in the most unlikely material, heavy tweeds in checks. We got into nicer quality merchandise eventually. It wasn't that long after post-war austerity in a way. Marcus knew people from the art school and the university. We saw a lot of students but they didn't seem to have as much money as students today. We were mostly selling to working-class lads who had money. City Stylish were our rivals, but they weren't much cheaper. Our Grey street shop was more up-market.

The best seller in the early 1960s was a strange and revolting pullover, knitted across ways with a batwing effect, with a basic body colour in red, black or mid blue and a stripe. It was called the Albatross. It sold very well, pre-Beatles. Before the Beatles came the scooter craze. The mod jacket was an Italian style, three button, short bum-freezer, usually in stripes, blue and grey, blue and black, brown and black and they sold like wildfire. Then was the famous Beatle jacket with round neck and buttons, sometimes shiny, and piped edges.

In May 1965 Bob Dylan came into the shop with Alan Price and a couple of others, to buy clothes. He was very well-mannered and polite and was very taken with a traditional black blazer with shiny buttons which he bought, plus a pink shirt and multi-coloured tie. The teenage assistants were very excited, but didn't hassle him for an autograph.

David Bell, manager of Marcus Price, Groat Market

(You can experience Bob Dylan's trip to Newcastle and his visit to Marcus Price on the deluxe edition of Bob Dylan's DVD *Don't Look Back*. Well worth a look!)

The Burton's Boys

Later on, when we got into fashion, my good friend Rob started working at Burton's and in those days you could go in and buy a made-to-measure suit with all the trimmings (pirate sleeves, very large centre vents, different collar styles, etc)on the never-never at two shillings a week. Usually by the time you finished paying off the suit you needed a new one. I remember one of the first times I wore a suit was a night out at the old Assembly Rooms on Gosforth High Street. It was spread over two storeys above some shops and it used to get packed. You had to climb the stairs to the first floor where the groups would play and on the next floor was the bar. In those days we were too young to drink so we stayed on the music floor, but I remember a

Blackett Street, 1 June, 1966. Burton's is on the corner opposite Cook's.

fight breaking out in the bar between two guys who managed to fight all the way down the stairs to the street below where they dusted themselves off, shook hands and then went back in. Unfortunately the Assembly Rooms were closed soon after that.

Another clothes shop was Marcus Price, a bit more pricey than City Stylish but more special. Marcus Price lived just round the corner from us, on Moorfield Road, and was always very dapper even though he was a lot older than us (he probably looked older as he didn't have much hair). His shop was down from Windows in the Central Arcade so it was very difficult for me not to go in both.

Mik Richardson

Style on a shoestring

We couldn't afford Biba or Mary Quant, so we trawled the jumble sales for 'something unusual', it didn't matter that we smelled of moth balls. 'That's original, it must be fashionable.' My friend and Kath and I thought we had arrived wearing our M & S stockings in Ecru, Sandalwood or American Tan. Tights were experimental at the time. At the discotheque, the danger with stockings lay in wearing odd ones, one white leg and one brown, and it was apparent who had only washed the feet as they resembled a shire horse.

We bought festooning billowy skirts from the sales, cut the waistband off, and voila, laid out the fabric and had a new dress. Kath was a perfectionist, she pinned, tacked and pressed her seams. I on the other hand needed to wear the creation that night, hence, one puffed sleeve and one flat, but hey!

The Journal, 1965

Petticoat was our favourite magazine, full of designs, make-up and free paper patterns. In one edition, another pal, Sandra, noticed a 'fab' tabard. She smuggled a very fine grey blanket from her mother's room, cut out her creation and chucked the remnants on the garden roof. She denied all knowledge of its disappearance, however, it became apparent what she had done on her return from the youth club that night. She was grounded for a week. No doubt her Mum would have discovered it anyway, the next time she had cleaned the landing window.

Fashion, for the first time was accessible to the youngster; other friends who hadn't quite caught up with us were still attempting to grapple a doll's dress onto the family cat, then pin it down with a blanket into a toy pram. There was a mix of Sandie Shaw hairstyles, or tatted hair, smooth at the front and like a bird's nest at the back, with 50s fashion still hanging on. A girl in our school yard wore a jumper; on the back, drawn in pen BEETLES, then an 'A' scribbled over the top of the second E. Everyone else pretended that they knew how it was spelled. We decorated our bags and shoes with nail varnish, we splashed ourselves with new fragrances – 'You don't say scent, say perfume!' Which was difficult when all we had was 5711.

We listened to our transistor radios, plucked our eyebrows within an inch of their lives, spat on mascara blocks, painted on lower eyelashes Twiggy style, a bit of Bourjois rouge and off to the Majestic. The music from Donovan, Stones, Beatles, Mary Hopkins, it didn't matter, everyone existed together in their own style, all dancing in our dodgy tights, smelly Afghan coats, swinging our beads, singing 'Yeah, Yeah, Yeah, Yeah'.

Yvonne Young

I had a white pique dress, thought I was the bee's knees. Someone said, 'that's nice material, you want to get a dress made out of that!'

Pauline Luke

TWAM

This op-art bag dates from 1963.

ncjMedia

To be stylish

City Stylish, near Cooks Corner, was the best for reasonably priced gear but for the really 'in crowd', especially those more financially sound, Marcus Price was a must. It was at about this time that labels started to matter, Ben Sherman shirts being at the pinnacle of 'cool'. Old men, those over 25, all had at least one suit and it was a made to measure one. Jackson the Tailor, Burtons, John Collier (the window to watch) had a presence in the town and whilst the suits were bespoke they all tended to look the same.

Joe Rogerson

Clothes were a big part of the culture. I bought a lot from City Stylish. I always remember buying a pair of checked hipsters (as worn by Roger Daltrey of The Who on the cover of the *My Generation* LP) and a grey polo neck jumper with what resembled a black and red scarf, which went round the top and down the back and the front. I also had a red shirt with a big collar and a gold design that that smelt as though it had been painted on. My mother just loved washing that shirt.

Mik Richardson

At the north end of Blackett Street, beyond its junction with Clayton Street, was the Anglo American Clothing Supermarket. Great for jeans.

'I remember splashing out 69s 11d on a Ben Sherman shirt at City Stylish for a boy I was courting at the time.' (Karin Musson)

Your mother should know

Most of the week I wore school uniform much of which was bought at Isaac Walton's. This was a very old-fashioned establishment. The assistant stood behind a long counter made of solid wood and selected the clothes from wooden shelves behind her. At first it was very exciting trying on the blazers, hats and ties – the thrill wore off as quickly as the newness! Items were soon 'customised' … the hat squashed and bent beyond recognition and the skirt shortened as much as you could get away with.

Fenwick's, Bainbridge's, British Home Stores and Marks & Spencer didn't really specialise

Isaac Walton, Grainger Street, 1970.

in clothes for teenagers. For these we usually went to C & A. I had a bright pink double-breasted coat – meant to be three-quarter length but I wore it as a fashionable 'mini' length, and a cotton suit which was white with big 'op-art' flowers all over it.

Fenwick's had a 'Pocket Money Casual' department where I bought a black-watch tartan shift dress which I wore with a black polo-neck sweater – cool! The Beatles popularised black polo-neck sweaters but it took me a long time to persuade my Mum to let me have one.

PVC became the 'in' material for all sorts of clothes including coats, skirts and even trousers. I had a short blue coat that fastened with metal fasteners. Paper dresses appeared for a short time – the novelty soon wore off – especially when it rained!

Jane Boyd (nee Turnbull)

An article in Newcastle Life, November 1966, above, featured the Fenwick boutique, Clobber. The model was Jenny Boyd, sister of Beatle George Harrison's wife Patti Boyd. Other boutiques mentioned include Elle, Target, Blaise, Scene and Tempo.

Left, Marks & Spencer, Prudhoe Street entrance.

105

These Boots are made for Walking

With the influence of Courreges and Mary Quant, boots became more fashionable than functional in the winter of 1962-3, and I had a lovely pair of mid-calf white leather boots purchased in Wengers, at the bottom of Grainger Street. Although they were for best I used to sneak out in them and they had a short but happy life with the heavy snowfall of that winter. I had knee-length brown boots for everyday wear

Parrish's, Shields Road, 1972.

and wore them to school one day where another girl and I were pulled into the Head's office and ordered home to change into something more suitable, such as wellington boots. As we wouldn't be seen dead in wellies we walked the two miles back to school in knee-deep snow wearing flat shoes and spent the day with soaking feet, but at least the rules had been observed.

In the early sixties Shields Road was a thriving shopping centre and that was where most residents of the East End of the City did their shopping. There were two department stores; Parrish's and Beavans and a shoe shop on practically every corner. My love affair with shoes started with a pair of white flatties with gilt chains bought for 17s 6d on Shields Road. The very first pair of shoes I bought myself was a pair of mock croc wedges from Manfield on the corner of Bigg Market and Grainger Street. I loved them so much I wanted to wear them to bed!

My mother was a very talented seamstress and when twist dresses became fashionable in 1963 she made them for most of my friends; we spent hours in the Silk Shop on Pilgrim Street choosing materials.

A friend and I decided to have a go at making skirts, but not knowing the first thing about dressmaking we bought the smallest amount of material possible and, because we wanted to wear them to the Majestic that night, we tacked up one seam and down the other. Great idea until we had to run to catch the bus to town and the seams started to part company, not very funny in front of a bus queue of people when you are 14 and think you look gorgeous.

That was not my only dressmaking disaster to involve a bus queue. My mother made me a skirt which buttoned up the front, and gave me the job of doing the buttons and buttonholes. I was in too much of a hurry to mess about with buttonholes so I used press studs and sewed the buttons on over them. This worked very well until I was waiting for the all night bus with my boyfriend outside Bowers and we had a row. I made to walk away and he grabbed at my skirt to stop me and it came off in his hand. I was left standing in my black leather jacket, stockings and suspenders in front of around 60 people! I was last seen heading up Pink Lane faster than the speed of light, quite appropriate given the reputation of Pink Lane!

June Sains

My favourite clothes around 1965-6 were grey checked wool hipster bellbottoms, with a wide red PVC belt from C & A. A friend had a fabulous black and purple striped trouser suit. My older brother, who shopped at Marcus Price or in London, wore a cool black PVC coat which I 'borrowed', though it was far too big. I longed for Levi's and saved up to buy khaki cords from Marcus Price. I wore a black polo neck Beatle jumper, and very short skirts which were much less embarrassing after tights appeared on the scene. At school there was an odd fashion for navy blue nylon macs, worn with dark brown stockings (the exact shade was 'calvados').

Newcastle Life

Newcastle Life, February 1967.

Around 1966 I bought two Biba dresses on a trip to London, short and bell shaped with bell sleeves, one flowered, the other brown check. I wore white stockings with them, and shoes with T bars. I had denim bell-bottoms with home-frayed fringes, beads and bells. Eye shadow was blue, eye lashes were black and heavy (like Marianne Faithful's). How I longed to impress the hippies in Handyside Arcade!

One winter outfit I was fond of in 1968 consisted of royal blue mini-culottes (rather like my hockey shorts), a yellow and black striped skinny-rib sweater (Fenwick's), navy blue kneesocks (over tights), worn with dark red shoes. I thought I was pretty sharp.

Anna Flowers

We'd go on the treadle sewing machine on a Saturday and run up a dress for the night. We got patterns from the Silk Shop. My mother used to say 'you've sewn that with a red hot needle. It'll fall apart!' Very short skirts… I was sitting by the fire in a friend's house, on a low stool and her mam said: 'Eee, our Jean, will you throw a tea towel over that lass's legs before your grandad has a heart attack!'

Pauline Luke

In 1966 I was still at school and fashion mad, though never able to buy in City Stylish or Bus Stop. My friend and I would walk to the town over Byker Bridge heading for Northumberland Street with not a penny in our pockets but we loved window shopping.

Most of my clothes were hand-me-downs from a rich cousin (well I thought she was) who was three years older. One dress I can never forget was a black and white check mini and I prayed when she was looking in the wardrobe that this dress would not fit her, in fact I went as far as to say this to her when she asked my opinion. To my great delight I was handed the dress, and I managed to save up for a black and white cap. I wore them with great pride when visiting the Oxford.

Linda Gray

It was around this time that my parents bought me a pair of red, winkle picker patent leather shoes…

Pam Wilson

1960s Newcastle

Clockwise from the right, Haymarket around 1960; Northumberland Street crowds, 1968; Eldon Square, 1968; Northumberland Street, 1968; Grainger Street, late 1960s.

Sunglasses, 1967.

Left, jumpsuit, bought around 1966. 'I loved the satin feel of the paisley fabric. I was given many compliments!'

Margaret Dinsdale

'We were all young, aged 15-19 and we had a love-in in Newcastle, gathering on the steps of the Mucky Angel (Haymarket war memorial) and progressing to the Handyside Arcade, more specifically the Beachcomber, a first floor café, where we hung out.

I lived in Wallsend and I remember a few neighbours coming on to their door steps to wave me off. I was wearing my Mother's old maternity smock, a huge floral affair. My mate was absolutely 'it' in her grandmother's peach silk pyjamas. Everyone wore beads and flowers and our long hair flowed. We didn't smoke anything stronger than Consulate menthol but we did think we were cool.'

Annie Moir

The Haymarket Angel, Autumn 1967.

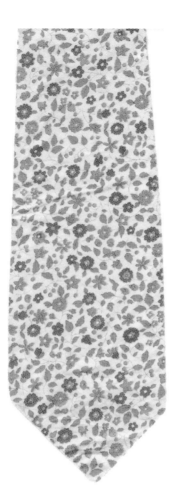

Did we really wear that?

The dress, above right, was made in 1968 from furnishing fabric.
The Afghan coat, right was bought in London, but worn in Newcastle.

Coral pink wool by
Biba, 1969.

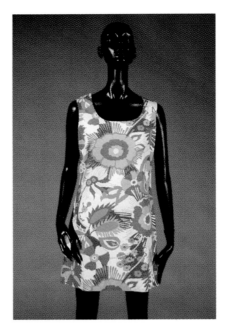

Mini-dress, 1969.

Black PVC coat
by Mary Quant,
and black leather
mini-skirt, 1965-
1969.

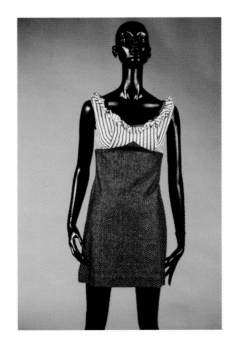

Dollyrockers
dress, 1966.

Biba coat, 1969.

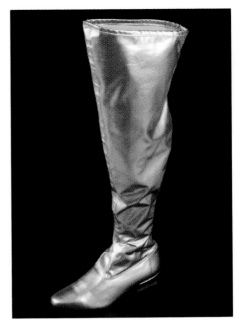

Sacha boot,
1965-1969.

A dress from
around 1960.

Waistcoat, 1969.

Chelsea boot, 1963.

Oxford winkle-picker, 1960.

Cord boot, 1965.

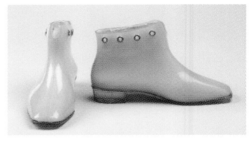

PVC boot by Mary Quant, 1965.

Moya shoe, 1965.

Satin shoes worn to La Dolce Vita, 1964.

Shoes by Lotus, 1964.

Saxone sandals, 1962.

Shopping in Heaton, 1968.

Handyside Arcade, late 1960s.

Percy Street and one of the entrances to Handyside Arcade, late 1960s. The Club A 'Gogo was on the top floor.

Briggflatts, published by Fulcrum Press, 1966.

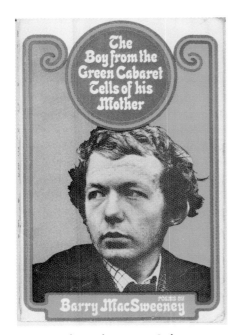

The Boy from the Green Cabaret,
published by Hutchinson, 1968.

Morden Tower, 1967.

Newcastle's vibrant poetry scene centred around the Morden Tower Bookroom, set up by Tom and Connie Pickard in 1964. Poet Basil Bunting gave the first reading of Briggflatts there on 22 December 1965. Young poet Barry McSweeney was inspired by the Tower. His first book was published in 1967. Tom Pickard's Ultima Thule bookshop was in Handyside Arcade.

CLUB AGOGO
PERCY STREET
1st FEB–7th FEB

MON – BIG DISC RAVE – 1/-
TUES – TOP TWENTY NITE – 1/-
WED – TOP SIX RECORDS
FREE RECORDS GIVEN AWAY.

OUTLINES* FREE TO GOGO MEMBERS* Y.S – 8/-

THURS – JUNCO PARTNERS*
FREE TO GOGO MEMBERS – Y.S – 8/-

FRI & SAT – THE FANTASTIC R&B SOUND
ALEX HARVEY SOUL BAND
WITH THE S/R R&B BILL OF
VONDYKES & DOWNBEATS
PRICES* FRI – 4/-&5/-* SAT – 5/-& 8/6

SAT – RETURN OF THE COLDS 2/6

CITY HALL, NEWCASTLE
Sunday. 6th November at 6.00 and 8.30 p.m.

Kennedy Street Enterprises Ltd. *in association with* Harold Davison and Tito Burns *present*

THE HOLLIES / SMALL FACES
PAUL & BARRY RYAN

PETER JAY & THE NEW JAYWALKERS ★ THE NASHVILLE TEENS ★ Robb STORME & the Whispers

Guest Star **PAUL JONES**

Compere for tonight's show — RAY CAMERON

5:-
7/6
8/6
10/6
12/6
Seat prices

HOLLIES—SMALL FACES SHOW

Book at A. E. Cook Ltd., Saville Place, Newcastle

POSTAL BOOKING SLIP

To A. E. Cook, Ltd., Saville Place, Newcastle
Please forward..........seats at........for the 6.00/8.30 performance on Sunday 6th November
I enclose stamped addressed envelope and P.O./Cheque value
NAME
ADDRESS

Hastings Printing Company, Drury Lane, St. Leonards-on-Sea, Sussex. Telephone Hastings 2450

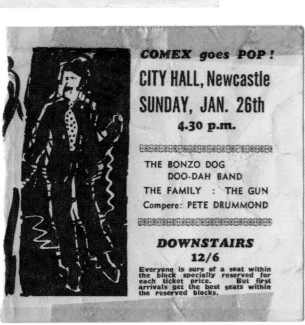

COMEX goes POP!

CITY HALL, Newcastle
SUNDAY, JAN. 26th
4.30 p.m.

THE BONZO DOG
DOO-DAH BAND
THE FAMILY : THE GUN
Compere: PETE DRUMMOND

DOWNSTAIRS 12/6

Everyone is sure of a seat within
the block specially reserved for
each ticket price. But first
arrivals get the best seats within
the reserved blocks.

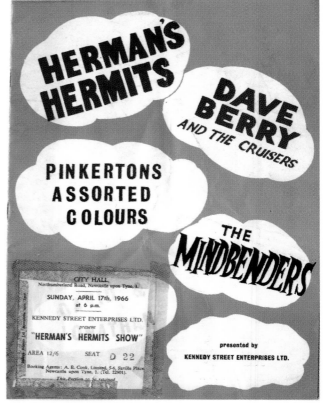

HERMAN'S HERMITS

DAVE BERRY AND THE CRUISERS

PINKERTONS ASSORTED COLOURS

THE MINDBENDERS

CITY HALL,
Northumberland Road, Newcastle upon Tyne, 1.
SUNDAY, APRIL 17th, 1966
at 6 p.m.
KENNEDY STREET ENTERPRISES LTD.
present
"HERMAN'S HERMITS SHOW"
AREA 12/6 SEAT D 22
Booking Agents: A. E. Cook, Limited, 5-6, Saville Place,
Newcastle upon Tyne, 1. (Tel. 22901).
This Portion to be retained

presented by
KENNEDY STREET ENTERPRISES LTD.

CITY HALL,
Northumberland Road, Newcastle upon Tyne, 1.

THURSDAY, 11th February, 1965
at 6.30 p.m.

ARTHUR HOWES
presents

The Cilla Black/P. J. Proby Show

AREA 10/6   SEAT   S 19

Booking Agents: A. E. Cook, Limited, 5-6, Saville Place,
Newcastle upon Tyne, (Tel. 22901).
This Portion to be retained.

PETER WALSH, KENNEDY STREET ENTERTAINMENTS LTD., & TITO BURNS present

DEL SHANNON

WAYNE FONTANA
and the
MINDBENDERS

the
SHANGRI-LAS

HERMAN's HERMITS

CITY HALL,
Northumberland Road, Newcastle upon Tyne, 1.

SUNDAY, 7th MARCH, 1965
at 6 p.m.

KENNEDY ENTERPRISES LTD.
presents

DEL SHANNON SHOW

AREA 10/6   SEAT   C 37

Booking Agents: A. E. Cook, Limited, 5-6, Saville Place,
Newcastle upon Tyne, (Tel. 22901).

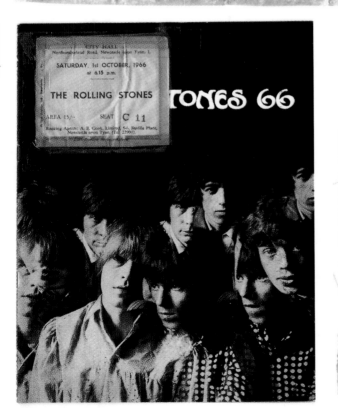

CITY HALL,
Northumberland Road, Newcastle upon Tyne, 1.

SATURDAY, 1st OCTOBER, 1966
at 6.15 p.m.

THE ROLLING STONES

AREA 15/-   SEAT   C 11

Booking Agents: A. E. Cook, Limited, 5-6, Saville Place,
Newcastle upon Tyne, (Tel. 22901).

TONES 66

CITY HALL,
Northumberland Road, Newcastle upon Tyne, 1.

THURSDAY, 6th MAY, 1965
at 7.30 p.m.

TITO BURNS
presents

BOB DYLAN

AREA 15/-   SEAT   N 14

Booking Agents: A. E. Cook, Limited, 5-6 Saville Place
Newcastle upon Tyne, (Tel. 22901).
This Portion to be retained.

BOOM BOOM · AROUND AND AROUND
DIMPLES · I'VE BEEN AROUND

mono

the animals

Columbia

EMI

The Animals, Newcastle's answer to Liverpool's Beatles. Their fame was intense, and although the original line-up was short-lived, their music lives on!

Boy Meets Girl boutique, Bigg Market, 1969.

Jobs for the girls

In 1961, my school friend Suzanne and I, aged 13, attended Victor Sylvester's Dance Studios in Gateshead for an hour's ballroom dancing class on Saturday mornings. After the class we might go to a coffee bar before catching the bus home to Chester-le-Street, but often Suzanne and I would walk across the bridge to Newcastle to window shop and plan what we'd spend our money on if we could get a Saturday job. I'd set my heart on a suede coat which would take a lot of saving up for.

We started asking in every shop we went in if they had any vacancies for Saturday girls. To our amazement the Personnel Manager in Bainbridge's agreed to see us. The conversation was going well and it looked as if we might get a job in the fashion department. This promising start came to a rapid end when she checked our application forms 'You're just 13!' she exclaimed 'Too young – come back in a couple of years'. Goodbye suede coat for the time being

Eventually I got a job in Eve Brown's in Northumberland Street. We sold ladies' dresses, coats and – best of all – bridal wear. We earned commission on sales and had a good staff discount. Because you could earn big commission on wedding finery, the full-time staff tried to keep the Saturday girls away from brides. However, if everyone was busy I jumped in quickly. Looking after brides-to-be, mothers and bridesmaids was a thrill. Helping them choose clothes, showing them into the large dressing room we kept for wedding customers, zipping up, arranging skirts and trains – a great experience for a girl not quite 15. Especially when they bought the wedding gown I'd picked out, with the veil and tiara – all that commission!

Unpacking boxes of new clothes was always a thrill, even if I had to press them by hand before they went out onto the sales floor. If I fancied something I could put it by until I'd earned enough commission to pay for it.

I decided not to buy one of the topless dresses that came out in the early 1960s! They usually had a

The largest shop in Newcastle

OVER 70 DEPARTMENTS

including Ladies' Hairdressing · Self Service
Food Market · Four Restaurants

BAINBRIDGE & CO. LTD., NEWCASTLE UPON TYNE, I
A Branch of The John Lewis Partnership

low square neckline that fitted under the bust. Most people wore a blouse underneath, but once I passed a woman walking down Northumberland Street in one 'au naturel'. Fortunately it was a warm day.

Another interesting experience was lunch time. We had early and late lunch times and I would always try to get on the same lunches as three of the older full-time staff. They'd probably be in their late twenties or thirties, but seemed to me to be very mature and knowledgeable about the ways of the world, especially when it came to Newcastle night life and men! We sat round the table in the staff room to eat our sandwiches and they'd tell us about their latest adventures – all of which were eye opening and hysterically funny.

There were two male managers who ran the shop. Both seemed to have regular lady clientele that they served personally – even to the extent of going into the fitting rooms with them. They seemed particularly attentive when topless dresses were the mode.

When business was quiet the managers would send the Saturday girls around the town with large Eve Brown carrier bags stuffed with polythene to look as if they were bulging with purchases. I'm not sure if this method of advertising enticed people in.

Yes, I did finally save up enough to buy the suede coat.

Tana Durham

Northumberland Street, and Eve Brown, early 1960s.

I got a Saturday job in Littlewood's store on Northumberland Street and worked in the lingerie/nightwear department. We got meal vouchers to eat at the canteen, for me a real novelty. Once a month I used to buy the latest single from Windows in Central Arcade and go to Marcus Price and buy flower power kit for my brother. Another treat was a Chinese meal with friends at The Sunrise Chinese Restaurant, down a spiral staircase below Emerson Chambers.

Lynn Jacobs

Littlewoods, Northumberland Street, 1967.

My first job was at Boots on Northumberland Street, Autumn 1969. Boots had the first escalator in the city and the old narrow wooden moving staircase was still in use. We wore grey checked overalls, no trousers allowed, and the endless standing at the tills was exhausting after being a schoolgirl. I got £6 a week and hated my job. I left at Christmas (to work in the University Library – what a joy, proper lunchbreaks). I would catch a smoky bus to my boyfriend's, miles away in Sunniside, from Marlborough Crescent, waiting in long queues as if we were in a cattle pen, freezing cold in a mini-skirt.

Anna Flowers

Newcastle was such a great place to be a teenager. I loved the Northumberland Street shops. Eve Brown's was one of the trendy ones. If my friend Eileen or I bought a coat from there, we thought we were the bees knees. Saxone's the shoe shop was on the corner and I remember looking in the window praying my Mam would buy me an expensive pair (69s 11d). Instead I always got them from Stylo up the street for 49s 11d. I started work in 1969 at the Co-op offices in Newgate Street. My first job was sorting pass books out when people got their yearly dividend. When I got my wages I made sure I went back to Saxone's and bought those 69s 11d shoes.

Saturday afternoons were spent hanging around the Arcade on Percy Street, full of hippie shops smelling of incense sticks, with hippie clothes and bangles. We would wander round to C & A to stare at the lovely leather and suede coats on the first floor. Even now when I smell suede or leather it brings back the smell of upstairs in C & A on a Saturday afternoon. When my mam finally bought me one, it was a huge treat – the expense of it – as my dad's wages were only £11 a week. I never heard the last of it, 'Look after that coat!' she would shout as I went out the door.

Karin Musson

The Raymond Yeast Ray Permanent Wave

I started a hairdressing apprenticeship when I left school and was lucky enough to go to Mortimer's on North Terrace, a beautiful high-class hairdressers. I got the job through the careers officer, Miss Calderwood, and three of us started at the same time. You were supposed to pay £100 fee to be an apprentice which was a huge amount of money but the careers office arranged that I wouldn't have to pay. I got 19s a week as an apprentice but my pay eventually went up to £2 10s.

Mortimer's training school was in Darlington and I had to travel there every day, paying my train fare out of my wages. If I'd been to the Downbeat I'd get home at 4am, then off to Darlington! We never felt tired. The standard was very high – I spent two months just learning to shampoo hair. When I first started hairdressing, people wanted styles that flicked up at the ends like Millicent Martin. We used big rollers to do that. Beehives, backcombing and pin curls were also popular. Blow drying was just becoming fashionable too. The Theatre Royal contracted us to look after the stars' hairstyles before shows. I had an assignment with the singer Vanessa Leigh.

I went to London to learn how to do a new type of perm. It was called the Raymond Yeast

Pauline Luke

Mortimer's staff demonstrate Raymond's Yeast Wave at Durant Hall around 1960.

Wave. You used wooden rollers and wheeled a machine with electric blue lights to the customer's chair to process the perm. Customers could buy a 21 guinea contract that allowed them to have as many perms as they liked in a year. We also offered tints and manicures.

Perms went out of fashion and straight hair was all the rage. People even ironed their hair! Then everybody wanted short, sculptured styles. Vidal Sassoon pioneered assymetrical cuts and that revolutionised the way we cut – mind not everyone could do it. It took a long time so it wasn't a good money spinner. Vidal Sassoon and Mary Quant came to do a workshop at the City Hall. That was wonderful. The platform came right out like a cat walk. Fantastic!

Pauline Luke

The Beehive

Shawn Fairless

Early morning memories from 1963 – my mother in her candlewick dressing gown, zipper up the front, with her beehive wrapped in toilet paper. This was supposed to keep it straight after a full night's sleep! She was very proud of her beehive as she put it up herself using a 'false piece' and enough hairpins to sink a battleship. She also kept a knitting needle handy though she couldn't knit to save her life. This was just to scatch her head if she had an itch!

Shawn Fairless

Department stores

Next door to each other on Market Street were two of my favourite shops; Binn's and Bainbridge's. Binn's was popular and usually very busy. It was also very grand with marble floors and a stunning marble staircase that was rumoured to have been imported from Italy and bankrupted Coxon's, the previous owners of the store. At the tea shop on the top floor waitresses in black dresses and white caps and aprons served customers at tables covered with pink linen cloths.

Next door was Bainbridge's, which was always considered rather more up-market. You entered the store through an impressive arcade with striking window displays. The main feature of the first floor was a gallery that overlooked the ground floor. Sadly the grand effect was spoiled by the netting that hung underneath the balustrade that surrounded the gallery – I assume it was there to stop items falling (or being dropped) onto the shoppers below.

Bainbridge's tea room was The Chattery and it certainly lived up to its name! Mornings and afternoons there were enlivened by fashion shows when models (possibly from Bainbridge's own staff, or perhaps from the Lucie Clayton School of Modelling in the Bigg Market) walked round the tables showing off the latest fashions from the ladies' wear department.

Many department stores had hairdressing departments, but I think Bainbridge's was the only one in Newcastle to offer the services of a chiropodist.

Round the corner on Grainger Street was another department store called Murton's. It had a very good childrenswear department called Mini Mode, where I found some lovely clothes for my two little girls.

Agnes Chilton

Binns, Market Street, 1967. The slogan on the back of the buses was always 'Shop at Binns'.

Try Farnon's Last

Farnons felt less salubrious than other department stores. It was further from the better shopping streets. It had some decent reasonably priced stock, though, mixed in with budget buys. The displays weren't as showy as other stores and I seem to remember plain wooden floors (not in a chic way) and old fashioned clothes rails with wheels. However after trailing the whole of Newcastle looking unsuccessfully for a particular item I often would remember their slogan and would try them last (usually at almost closing time). It frequently worked and I got what I wanted. I bought my 'going away' hat there, then did a couple of minor alterations to it. It just wasn't the sort of shop you would think to try first.

Tana Durham

Farnon's, Nun Street, with its unusual but effective slogan 'Try Farnon's last', late 1960s.

arcadia

Handyside Arcade on Percy Street was an airy three-storey Victorian shopping arcade with a glass roof held up by cast iron pillars. It was home to the Henry Osborne tool shop, a canteen and sub-depot for the Corporation buses and the famous Club A 'Gogo.

Geoff Laws

I bought a lovely outfit in one of those shops. It was blue and green dogtooth with a cap, made by Suzy, she was very arty.

Pauline Luke

Handyside Arcade, 1967. Over the years shops included Kard Bar, Scene, Blaise, Figleaf, Target, Beautique, Pot, Kaleidoscope, Muffin, Object, Suzy's, and Witches Coffee Bar. There was also an alternative bookshop Ultima Thule (to the right of this photograph), run by poets Tom Pickard and Tony Jackson.

Handyside Arcade, 1970.

Handyside's Arcade became Arcadia and it became a
weekend hippy hang out with trendy clothes shops,
places to buy joss sticks and a hippy bookshop
called Ultima Thule run by a local beat poet. There
was also Kard Bar, which sold posters, cards and
all sorts of ephemera. I got to know the owner
Brian Sandles. I was still at college at the time
and he gave me my first commission to design
a poster of the band T Rex to sell in his shop.
At that time there were just two of them,
Marc Bolan on guitar and percussionist Steve
Peregrine Took.

Geoff Laws

I remember going to the Oxford Sale Rooms beside the Laing Art Gallery with Dad. The
big doors were open and people spilled out onto the street, there were seats inside and the
Auctioneer/salesman stood with his gavel on the stage surrounded by the items for sale. One sale I
remember was in 1966, when dad bought a new dinner service and my brother and I were bought Batman
and Robin outfits. The series was a big favourite and the film had just been released. I, being the
youngest, got Robin.

There was a chemist, which was known as Dirty
Dicks. I cannot remember where in Newcastle it was
but would love to find out, it was like stepping into
an old apothecary's shop. As a child I had an
enormous wart on my left hand. All manner of
creams had been used to no avail, then an aunt said
'take him to Dirty Dicks, he'll get rid of it.' This my
parents did. It was like stepping into an old
apothecary's shop; it had the usual jars of glucose
and licorice sticks, licorice root on a high dark wood
counter. My left hand was presented to, I presume,
Mr Dick who took one look and proceeded to make

Dirty Dick's, Clayton Street. There was no Mr Dick!

a mixture from the brown bottles that lined the walls behind the counter. The mixture was then handed over and was to be taken orally! After two or three weeks the wart, itching like mad, was gone.

On many a Sunday the family would go to the Quayside Market which always had crowds of people. The stall holders entertained us with their cries of, I'm not asking £2 10s, I'm not asking £2 2s 6d, £2 the lot, come on ladies and gentlemen! And there were street entertainers, the sword swallower, the strong man bending an iron bar around his neck and the juggler.

Brian Thompson

Shields Road

Perhaps it was because I was a small boy and the fact that the journey from Walker to Scotswood on the 21 bus to visit relations was like going to the end of the earth, but Shields Road in Byker seemed a magical place when I was growing up in the 60s.

Byker Bridge, 1966.

Carter's pies, the like of which I have never tasted since. The Hadrian supermarket, with its upstairs café and gigantic windows, was where I would sit with my Dad on a Saturday morning and watch for people that we knew, passing in the street below. Occasionally I would stand outside The Raby, on the corner of Shields Road and Raby Street, while my dad went in to see my Granda – I'd be summoned in and quickly sent out again with two shillings or perhaps half a crown in my hand.

My favourites of course were the many toy shops. Thom's, two Hopkirk's. You didn't necessarily have to buy anything. Standing outside, gazing at the window displays, dreaming of that box of soldiers or an Airfix fighter plane was enough. Mind you, getting something was better. At Parrish's toy department, in the basement, I would always be treated to something whenever my Nana, Mam or Auntie Val got some Parrish's cheques. And of course Beavan's was perhaps the grandest of them all.

Robin Sword

Shopping on credit

Byker in the early 60s was bustling, it even had two department stores, Beavan's and Parrish's. Everything was there, the town was somewhere you made only a special visit to. Parrish's was noted for having its own currency, which could be bought on credit. Credit at least in Byker was the only way for most people to survive. The even less well off resorted to selling on the credit notes, known as orders or tickets, they were obtained from money lenders for half their face value. These 'half orders' were used for 'luxuries' such as clothing bought at shops such as Waterloo House, Roland Blaylocks, Wengers and Shepherds of Gateshead and all you had to do was to remember whose name the order was in. It took me some time to understand why my mam had so many surnames.

Joe Rogerson

Our mam loved shopping at the Co-op; her dividend number was either 2457 or 24577. We used to go there when we had a bit of extra money (which was not often) but her face used to light up when we needed to visit the Co-op. I was always fascinated when you needed change; your money would be placed in a container that was put into something that looked like a drain pipe and this was shot up through various pipes all over the ceiling to an office above. There someone would put your change back into the container and it came zooming back to you at great speed. My friend and I would go window shopping up and down Shields Road 'bagsing' this item and that one, taking turns of course.

Linda Gray

The Co-op supermarket, Newton Road, Heaton, at the end of the 1960s.

The supermarket

In the sixties I worked New Bridge Street in a supermarket called Broughs. I started there when I left school at 15; we wore white overalls and a white band around our heads, with the letter B on the front.

I worked on the check-out. I remember we had a delicatessen where we sold sandwiches, cold meats and cheeses. The local shop workers used to come in and get their lunches. The BBC studios used to be across the road and sometimes the newsreaders came into the shop, still wearing their orange TV make up.

Ellen Pennings

The Bigg Market was the spot for protesters and preachers as well as a market. On Tuesdays, Thursdays and Saturdays, stalls would be set up right down the Cloth Market for the sale of fruit, vegetables, clothing and gift items.

Small DIY shops were plentiful, supplying lunchtime shoppers with nails, screws and so on. There was one in the Bigg Market, Aynsley's in Percy Street, one in Darn Crook, another in the Grainger Market.

Broughs, New Bridge Street, around 1969.

I remember the fascination of the pneumatic tube system in Bainbridge's department store, on a maze of different levels between Market Street and the Bigg Market. Your money whizzed away in a small cylinder through tubes to reappear shortly afterwards with the correct change.

David Hughes

Right, confusing traffic arrangements at Grey's Monument roundabout, around 1968. Mawson Swan's is on the left on Grey Street.

Opposite, Haymarket bus station, July 1966.

Traffic misery

Northumberland Street was remarkable for its traffic. In the sixties it was still the A1, The Great North Road and one of the worst traffic jam blackspots. With narrow pavements and traffic running in both directions, both motorists and shoppers suffered equal misery. Crossing Northumberland Street was not a decision to take lightly. Did you really want to be on the other side? Would you want to cross back again soon? Would crossing now be worth the effort involved? Dodging between cars, buses, lorries, petrol tankers, etc made shopping a nightmare, especially at Christmas. The crowds around Callers' Christmas window display were huge and outside Fenwick's the narrow pavements were crammed with people like the crush at St James' Park after a football match. Eventually two pedestrian bridges were built over Northumberland Street, but it took the creation of John Dobson Street (not a fitting memorial to Newcastle's greatest architect and rather unkindly requiring the demolition of two churches that Dobson had designed) and then the Central Motorway East before people on foot regained the freedom they had before the motorcar took over the city streets.

Marlborough Crescent and Worswick Street bus stations were big and cavernous like aircraft hangers, full of pigeons. Buses were full (and everyone smoked) and it was not uncommon for passengers to stand all the way into Newcastle or even for buses to flash their lights and refuse to stop altogether. Long queues and full buses belching out black smoke amongst black buildings amid a constant, almost deafening, chatter from thousands of starlings that descended upon Newcastle at night.

Pedestrian streets were an unheard of luxury. Roads as wide as possible with multiple traffic lanes in a forlorn attempt to make room for all the cars wishing to move through the city. Sometimes the trolley buses would stop and the electric power pickups would be moved with a long pole to allow the bus to alter its route.

David Hughes

Trolley bus wires (for the No. 33) and a traffic policeman, Jesmond Road, 1966.

The junction of Northumberland Street and New Bridge Street was popularly known as 'Cook's Corner'. The footbridge was one of two erected in Northumberland Street in 1967 to help pedestrians avoid the often treacherous traffic. They didn't last long, people didn't bother to use them. The Pearl Assurance Building which housed Thos. Cook didn't last much longer either.

Leader of the pack

Budget motoring in the sixties centred on the bubble car and I lashed out £60 on a red Isetta three-wheeled machine, which was powered by a 350cc BMW side engine. It even had a canvas sun roof and could seat three skinny passengers at a pinch.

The entire front opened up, complete with attached steering wheel and the gear stick protruded from the right hand wall. Contrary to popular belief at the time, the Isetta also had a reverse gear. Although safety was not a high priority due to the eggshell thin fragility of the body, fuel economy was a major plus and it was possible to travel from Newcastle to Darlington and back on half a gallon. The big drawback was that after offering lifts to young ladies, they were less than impressed when a bubble car clattered down their street.

The sixties was also the age of the banger. I travelled the country in a £35 Austin A40 which I would now not dare to drive around the block. It had £2 retread tyres, no passenger front seat because the floor wouldn't support one, a broken rear leaf spring and a body so full of holes it looked like it had been on a wartime bombing run. When it went the journey I bought a green £50 Morris Minor with split screen windscreen and an unfeasibly long gear stick. I vividly recall stopping at a roundabout and watching in horror as the front wheel broke off and rolled around the roundabout by itself.

When I advertised the car for sale for £17 a pair of lads turned up at the house on foot and were closely followed by two blokes in a mini. They both glanced at the Morris and then did a deal over its bonnet for the mini for £25.

Tony Henderson

Tony Henderson

Tony Henderson and bubble car, around 1968. He failed his driving test in it as the windows were too small for hand signals.

Worswick Street bus station in 1971.

The last electric train

The chances are that if you can remember where you were at 6.14 pm on Saturday 17th June 1967, you will have been with me, awaiting the departure of the 6.15 pm 'all stations' service from platform 3 at Newcastle Central Station. It was the last journey in public service for one of the green electric trains of the North Tyneside line between Newcastle and the Coast. For over 60 years the line had been served by two fleets of rolling stock, the original set from 1904 to 1937 and their replacements from 1937 to 1967. The 'last train' travelled outwards via Wallsend, returning via Jesmond but of course the line operated simultaneously in both directions. The usual journey time was 58 minutes and the 'electrics' were known for their meticulous timekeeping, but on this occasion, with a lot of cheering and booing and an assortment of wreaths and solemn mutterings at stations all along the line the 20.5 miles were covered in a leisurely 78 minutes.

An electric train leaves Central Station for the coast, 1957.

It was amazing the train could make progress at all such was the volume of passengers on board. I remember standing for the entire journey and many 'ordinary' passengers at the suburban stations chose to await the following service rather than join the hoard of railway enthusiasts and well-wishers crammed in with us!

The electrics dominated the line during my years travelling on it, and they had their own distinctive characteristics. The bucket seats offered a good level of comfort whilst the doors were of the manual sliding variety. These allowed for shorter station stops which, coupled with the smooth acceleration of the electric engines, meant timekeeping was very consistent. I don't ever remember 'leaves on the line' being an issue then, even in winter time!

British Railways in the 1960s was in the grip of modernisation with the infamous Beeching Plan in operation. The image of the electrics was out-dated, and they had to be replaced, pronto! Although only 30 years old and fully maintained and serviced, the old had to make way for the new and this came in the form of diesel multiple units (known simply as DMUs). Cast-offs from other lines, they quickly showed their limitations; they were slow away from stations and the doors had to be closed individually. Overnight the timetable had to be changed, with longer station stops and slower acceleration proving their unsuitability on this testing commuter route. Modernisation equalled slower trains! Very quickly their days were numbered too. The new regime was on the drawing board and electrics would soon be returning, in the smart new yellow and white format of the Metro.

Godfrey Valentine

The night bus

Getting home after a night out was always a problem as the pubs and cinemas shut at 10.30 and the last buses left at 11pm. Taxis were never considered so the only option was the all night bus from Central Station which covered all of the east side of the city. I think there was one for the west as well but can't be sure as we were all very parochial, and interested in only our side of the town. This all changed when old Byker was pulled down and lots of the residents moved to new developments in the countryside (by which I mean Longbenton). It was the same I think for Scotswood but their Utopias (well at least the houses had bathrooms) were the likes of Newbiggin Hall.

Joe Rogerson

After a night out we'd go on to Bowers, opposite the Central Station which was open all night, although you did have to spend at least 2s 6d to be allowed in – chipolata and chips and a coke were the order of the night. If you couldn't make it through the night, the all-night bus ran at half-hourly intervals, one to the east and next one to the west of the City. Transportation was excellent in the 60s, loads of buses running regularly and a very efficient train service to the coast and all points in between. You could never blame the buses if you were late for work.

June Sains

The Haymarket bus station, late 1960s.

HALF-TIME SCOREBOARD   **NUMBER ONE**

A	MAN. CITY / MAN. UTD.	**F**	LEEDS UTD. / FULHAM	**L**	BLACKBURN / WOLVES
B	BLACKPOOL / ARSENAL	**G**	LEICESTER / SUNDERLAND	**M**	BOLTON / CARDIFF
C	CHELSEA / ASTON VILLA	**H**	LIVERPOOL / SOUTHAMPTON	**N**	CARLISLE / IPSWICH
D	TOTTENHAM / BURNLEY	**J**	SHEFF. UTD. / STOKE	**P**	MIDDLESBORO / SCUNTHORPE
E	WEST BROM. / EVERTON	**K**	WEST HAM / SHEFF. WED.		

HALF-TIME SCOREBOARD   **NUMBER TWO**

A	BIRMINGHAM / PRESTON	**F**	NORWICH / BURY	**L**	DONCASTER / Q.P.R.
B	BRISTOL CITY / COVENTRY	**G**	PLYMOUTH / NORTHAMPTON	**M**	GRIMSBY / BRIGHTON
C	CHARLTON / HUDDERSFIELD	**H**	PORTSMOUTH / ROTHERHAM	**N**	MANSFIELD / DARLINGTON
D	DERBY / CRYSTAL P.	**J**	BOURNEMOUTH / GILLINGHAM	**P**	PRESTON RES. / NEWCASTLE RES.
E	HULL / MILLWALL	**K**	COLCHESTER / OXFORD		

HALF-TIME SCOREBOARD   **NUMBER THREE**

A	PETERBORO / LEYTON	**F**	WALSALL / TORQUAY	**L**	HALIFAX / TRANMERE
B	READING / WATFORD	**G**	BARNSLEY / ALDERSHOT	**M**	HARTLEPOOL / BRADFORD CITY
C	SHREWSBURY / OLDHAM	**H**	BRADFORD / CREWE	**N**	NEWPORT / WREXHAM
D	SWANSEA / WORKINGTON	**J**	BRENTFORD / SOUTHEND	**P**	NOTTS CO. / YORK CITY
E	SWINDON / BRISTOL ROV.	**K**	CHESTER / BARROW		

NEWCASTLE UNITED
Black and White Striped Shirts
Black Shorts

1 Gordon Marshall
2 Ollie Burton
3 Frank Clark
4 Dave Elliott
5 John McNamee
6 John McGrath
7 Bryan Robson
8 Albert Bennett
9 Wyn Davies
10 Jim Iley *(Capt.)*
11 Tommy Robson
12

NOTTINGHAM FOREST
Red Shirts
White Shorts

1 Peter Grummitt
2 Peter Hindley
3 John Winfield
4 Terry Hennessey
5 Bob McKinlay
6 Henry Newton
7 Barry Lyons
8 John Barnwell
9 Joe Baker
10 Frank Wignall
11 Ian Storey-Moore
12

Referee : Mr. D. LAING, *Preston*
Linesmen: Red Flag: Mr. L. MEADOWS, *Redcar*
Yellow Flag: Mr. B. HUTCHINSON, *Leeds*

Any alteration to these teams will be announced over the loudspeakers

Football programme, 1967. Right, St James' Park, 1965.

GAMES PEOPLE PLAY

Get me to the match on time.

As a microscopic 12-year-old, it wasn't easy for me and some of my diminutive pals to see much amid the clamour of 50,000 animated Geordies packing the terraces. Our only hope of a decent view was to be installed inside St James' Park, at least an hour before kick-off time, which in those pre-satellite TV days, was always three o'clock.

If I was still in the chip shop when the clock went past noon, I knew my schedule was in jeopardy, but nothing was allowed to interfere with the match day ritual unfurling in the correct sequence and maximising the chance of two precious points later in the day. It was always fishcakes, chips and mushy peas for dinner, consumed wearing the obligatory lucky shirt, underpants and socks that had to be assembled in the correct sequence. The mode of transport never deviated. The number 32 trolley bus from Wallsend boundary could shift a bit, but had a habit of divorcing itself from the overhead power supply and easing to a halt halfway through Byker. With a bit of luck the conductor would have us back on track with the judicious use of a long pole, without threatening our precious timetable.

In those days the entrance charge for boys was a shilling although grown ups had to pay twice as much to see their heroes in action. Because of this disparity, and the acute shortage of 'boys' turnstiles, the juvenile queue would always stretch for ever, condemning us to a wait of at least half an hour outside the ground.

During this time, in addition to anticipating the delights to follow, we occupied ourselves by avoiding the marauding police horses who kept us in line, and speculating about how many 'boys' had forgotten to shave that morning! A turnstile designated for 'girls' was conspicuously absent.

Once through the turnstile and inside the hallowed portals it was time to implement the tried and tested viewpoint strategy. This entailed sprinting to the back of the 'popular side' aiming to get as near the half way line as possible, and then precariously clambering onto a fence made out of vertical railway sleepers. By standing on this 9ft wide platform and hanging on to overhanging trees, we had as good a view as the season ticket holders and directors in the wooden stand opposite, except that they could sit down and were protected from the elements.

Come rain hail or shine, Arsenal, Manchester United or Sunderland, we would be there, defying gravity and revelling in the silky skills of Ivor Allchurch and Len White until the final whistle would hopefully herald yet another win for our beloved Magpies.

Jim Holmes

St James' Park, 1963.

Back in those days you could turn up at the football and pay at the turnstiles. We must have got through the boys' entrance until we were all about 21! Our scarves were used as disguises.

Mik Richardson

Saturday afternoon at St James' Park – these were the days when the terraces were packed and the atmosphere was electric. The lad in the white smock would come around shouting 'nuts, tanner a bag'. It was amazing to see the tanners being thrown down to him and he would 'hoy' the bag up deep into the crowd – no complaints, he got his money and the buyer always got his bag of nuts. Visiting supporters were often mixed into the crowd and, yes, there were fights, but often between Toon fans – the football was hard, sometimes not that great, but the players always tried, and Geordie fans loved commitment above all else. Leaving a United match in those days was an experience too. The crush was that tight you could lift your feet off the floor and travel 20 yards, your chest getting tighter and tighter. Just when you started to get a little worried, you would suddenly be released – it was sometimes a close call.

Ray Marshall

My first taste of football at St James' Park was season 1960-61 when, utterly predictably, Newcastle United plunged into the Second Division, conceding 109 goals – their worst ever against tally. Astonishingly, this did not put me off and a lifetime of United ups, but mostly downs, has followed.

I remember, on my paper round, seeing a cartoon on the back page of the *Daily Express*, which pictured the Newcastle keeper standing between posts equipped with goal meters. How that hurt. Those were the days of corncrakers – the wooden rattles which would now be classed as an offensive weapon. Mine cost 10s 6d from Stan Seymour's sports shop and I have it to this day, with most people mistaking it for a medieval agricultural implement.

Us kids used to sit on a concrete wall which bordered the cinder track around the St James' pitch. Brass and pipe bands would provide the half time entertainment. When the kilted bagpipe players marched past, kids would lick fruit gums and refreshers and stick them to the pipers' hairy legs. After a few circuits they were well and truly covered.

Tony Henderson

From the age of eleven I was hooked on Newcastle United. My dad was a gateman. I stood in the paddock next to the tunnel and got first glimpse of all the stars as they came onto the field. School holidays were spent going to the training ground, then on Barrack Road, watching the team train then trying to get as may autographs as possible. My hero was Bryan 'Pop' Robson. We won the Fairs Cup in 1969, a great climax to end the decade.

Lynn Jacobs

I remember arriving at the top of the terrace at the Gallowgate End at about quarter past one for a three o'clock kick off. I was only seven or eight at the time and used to get the 39 or 40 bus from Roman Avenue in Walker to Gallowgate bus station. I had to get there really early so that I could find a place where I could climb up and sit on one of the barriers, just so I would be able to see. The barriers on the Popular Side and in the Leazes End were made of thin, round, yellow steel and you could never sit or even balance on one of them for a couple of hours. The Gallowgate End, however, had flat concrete barriers, sort of pebble dashed and scratchy but wide enough for my skinny backside.

My most vivid memories are not always of the game and players but of things that went on around me – anxiously waiting for that bus in Walker just wanting to get to the ground. *Hey Jude* being played over the public address system to an almost empty stadium as I arrived early to get my spot. The dark nights and queuing forever to get a bus home after a Wednesday night game. Queuing on the cobbles on Strawberry Lane with a sleeping bag and a flask of cocoa to get tickets for the Fairs Cup final. Perhaps best of all though was the fact that my Auntie Val worked in Billy Botto's betting shop on Prudhoe Street where some of the players would go after training. I still have that old betting slip bearing the autograph of my hero 'The Mighty Wyn' Davies.

Robin Sword

Newcastle United win the Fairs Cup, 1969. Frank Clarke holds the trophy and Bobby Moncur is in the foreground.

Speedway

In 1963 and 1964 we used to go to Brough Park, The Fossway, every other Monday night to watch the speedway (dirt track motor bike racing). I was only 13 or 14 at the time and I remember getting in for half price.

As soon as you got inside you could feel the charge in the air. The Buzz! The excitement! It was held in the winter months, or that's what I remember. It was always freezing cold. We used to be wrapped up like Michelin men and our breath made steam clouds when we talked, or rather shouted at each other. The noise of the event was hard to compete with but we were young and not easily defeated!

The track was inside the greyhound track. It was a narrow oval, famous for its tight bends and a rider seemed to have a near death experience just about every week. That's how I remember it, but I don't think there were any serious accidents.

The team was the Newcastle Diamonds. They wore black leathers with large white diamonds on the breast. I can't remember a lot about the individuals although Ivan Mauger was my never-to-be-forgotten favourite.

Annie Moir

Opposite, Newcastle University, 1964.

THE STUDENT LIFE

I came to Newcastle in September 1968 to start a degree in Agricultural Engineering at the University. It was my first encounter with the North East. I have never wished to live anywhere else.

The location of the University, right in the heart of the city, is marvellous. I liked being able to walk out of a lecture and within minutes be in the middle of town. The Haymarket pub was a favourite for a lunch time drink and a bun (cheese and onion of course). It had a warm fire, a cosy back room and a friendly atmosphere. It was novel to order 'a pint of scotch'. I never took to Exhibition Ale – too sweet. Brown Ale was also a favourite tipple, but not at lunch time due to its soporific properties.

An almost unrecogniseable view of the Students' Union building from Barras Bridge in March 1966. The Presbyterian Church is still there, with other university property and the University Theatre was yet to be built.

Students were not popular everywhere so it was wise to be a little cautious in a few places but I never received any threats or abuse. We were certainly privileged compared with today's students – and with many young people in the city at the time. The maximum state grant was £360 per year. This was more or less enough to live on for the academic year and did not have to be repaid later.

On Saturday nights there was a dance in the University Union. There was always a good atmosphere. I thought it was great fun to listen to an exciting band, have a few too many drinks and bop around – I still do. I also, from time to time, visited clubs in the town. Grey's Club was the one that I particularly liked. In those days it was split into a number of linked rooms. A decent band pumped out popular songs in the main room. There was a small disco in the brick walled cellar and another bar with a more intimate atmosphere. The owner was a former pop singer, David Macbeth. People in the club were very tolerant towards a young outsider with a posh accent.

The Town Moor was another part of Newcastle I really liked. It was invigorating to do a brisk walk over the wide expanses of the moor in the lunch break. The golf course shared the eastern section of the moor with some inquisitive cows. We used to sneak on for a few holes without paying but I can't remember being challenged by the long suffering members. The course was kept in surprisingly good condition considering the abuse it had to endure from not very skillful student golfers.

I tried, not very successfully, to appreciate the fine buildings of Newcastle. They were all covered by a thick carpet of black soot. Grey Street and the other fine buildings in the city were not revealed in all their rich sandstone glory until they were cleaned in the 1970s.

John Wilson

Ragweek

I was a student at Newcastle Art College from 1965 to 1969. In those days the college was housed in various buildings throughout the city. The fine art department was in what had been a magnificent old coal board office in Ellison Place, pretty much where the new footbridge over the central motorway now stands. The General Studies department was in a building on Northumberland Road. A Victorian school on Chillingham Road in Heaton contained the

A student rag stunt in the Haymarket in July 1961.

Graphic Design department and the Industrial Design department, in which I spent three years, was in a big old villa on Clayton Road in Jesmond. Eric Burdon had studied at Clayton Road several years before I went there and Ray Jackson (Jacka), singer and harmonica player for the band Lindisfarne was a contemporary of mine. The year after I left, the art college combined with Rutherford Technical College to become the Polytechnic and moved into the new campus on Sandyford Road.

An annual event in the student calendar was Rag Week, during which we roamed the shopping streets of Newcastle, dressed bizarrely, collecting money for charity in buckets. The highlight of the week was a procession that started behind the Central Station and slowly wound its way through the city centre ending up at Exhibition Park. The route included Northumberland Street before it was pedestrianised and was still the very busy A1 trunk road. Can you imagine the traffic chaos on a Saturday morning if they did it now?

The procession consisted mainly of decorated flat-bed lorries, but being art and design students we decided to come up with something different.

We took a Ford Prefect belonging to one of the students and changed it into what looked like a weapon of mass destruction powered by steam with a boiler, a chimney and a spinning fly wheel. We named it The Ultimate Deterrent, a well-used phrase in the days of the cold war.

The Rag Shop, Percy Street, 1969.

To build it we took anything that came to hand, cardboard tubes, tin cans, aluminium foil, plastic cups and in the end there was no sign of the car apart from the wheels and you had to climb in through the window. I'm quite surprised that the police let us drive it.

Hidden in the boot, accessed through a door in the back boiler, an unfortunate female student had the task of winding an old air-raid siren to create an ear-splitting whine as we went along. She probably suffered lasting effects. A row of metal cylinders, hanging down in front and clanking along the road, added to the cacophony.

It was probably one of the better designs that we came up with during our time at college.

Geoff Laws

Geoff Laws

The Ultimate Deterrent on the road.

Getting through the rubble

In 1965 I became a mature student at Newcastle Teacher Training College at Brady and Martin's old pharmaceutical warehouse on Northumberland Road. About 250 students milled about on the three floors of that death trap of a building. The upper floors were accessed by open wooden stairways which were only marginally sturdier than ladders. I drove from High Heaton each day and parked on waste ground in Shieldfield. After picking my way over the rubble-strewn ground, I reached Chester Street where I passed two survivors from Victoria's day, Temperance Row and Sanitary Place (they don't name streets like that any more). After turning right at the Prince of Wales pub I was at the end of Northumberland Road. No flyover walkways or motorways to contend with, just a straight walk up the road to my alma mater.

Joan Davidson

Rebuilding Newcastle, 1968.

The Beat Goes On

As the 1950s gave way to the 1960s I was one of the constables of the old Newcastle City Police patrolling the beats of the west side of the city on foot – no cars, no radios, no mobile phones. We supported each other and contact with the station was by a telephone from police boxes placed in prominent positions around the city.

We saw birth and death at close quarters, sadness, joy, anxiety, celebration, anger, the effects of drunkenness, many funny things; all the range of human emotions.

We had close contact with the other emergency services, particularly the fire brigade. At the beginning of the 1960s, the principal stations at Headlam Street, Pilgrim Street and the West Road were all joint stations for fire and police services.

It was the early hours of the morning, on a beat including part of Scotswood Road as it used to be. The night was fine and fairly quiet at that late hour, but there was something amiss because the lights of the district would flicker from time to time. Passing the showroom of a firm dealing in agricultural machinery, I realised there was an acrid smell in the air suggesting fire – but there was no smoke. After checking around I discovered the pavement was too hot to touch! The police box at the foot of Gloucester Street was nearby but I felt some trepidation in calling the fire service from their beds. Could there really be a fire without smoke? They came down to Scotswood Road, unimpressed, however when the senior fireman touched the pavement as I had done there was swift action.

Out came crowbars, the paving slabs were lifted, the fire crew dug down and a potential disaster was averted. There was a fault in an electrical cable beneath

Barry Redfern

Gloucester Street and the police box, early 1960s.

149

the pavement, causing great heat. The other problem was the gas main under the same pavement!! Turning off the electricity supply quickly reduced the heat and by the time my shift ended gangs of electricity and gas supply workers had been called out and were digging around the site to inspect and make things safe. The 'fairly quiet night' turned into something quite different.

Another day I was working the beat around the station. I walked out of the front door of the police station in the middle of the afternoon to hear a commotion a few hundred yards along the West Road away from the city. It was the racket of a vehicle horn

The West End Police Station, 1964.

continuously sounding, and I could see smoke amongst the traffic. I pressed the emergency bell at the fire station door and two firemen came out, looked at me and said 'What do you want?' I pointed up the West Road and said 'There's a fire on the way to the fire station.' Smoke rising from a moving vehicle was clearly visible now. One of the firemen uttered two words that cannot be repeated here and dashed into the fire tender garage. He emerged carrying a portable fire extinguisher just as an ice-cream van pulled onto the forecourt. Smoke was pouring out of the electrical cooling unit at the back of the ice-cream van. No one was hurt, the firemen quickly put out the fire and the vehicle was saved.

I have never heard of another example of the fire being brought to the fire station and I am glad I was there to see it!

Barry Redfern

Standing in the queue

I was 12 and living in Benwell at the start of the 60s and just beginning to be allowed into the city centre on a Saturday with schoolfriends. I think one of our first adventures (and we were so excited!) was to go to the pictures at the Haymarket to see Cliff Richard in *The Young Ones* in 1961. When we got there the queue was right round the corner up St Thomas's Street and we soon started to get hungry. I remember I went back home to Benwell and my Mam made a pack of sandwiches for me to take back to the pals!! (I don't think we bought food in town then or perhaps we just didn't want to leave the queue.)

Gail Richardson

If we had a few extra pennies we might go to the cinema – the flicks as we used to call it. *The Sound of Music* (my favourite film, to this day) was on at the Queens Cinema. It was the classiest cinema in Newcastle; the big screen made you feel you were in the Tyrol. The Queen's was along a little lane that led off Northumberland Street.

I also remember queuing to see *Help*, the Beatles film with my mother at the Odeon on Pilgrim Street. Being a big Beatles fan (I still am) I was so excited. I screamed all the way through the film, to my mother's annoyance, and her words outside were, 'That was the biggest load of rubbish I've ever paid for'.

Karin Musson

The pictures were in the main the only reason to go to town as everything else you needed was available in Byker where I was born and brought up. The Essoldo, Haymarket, Queens all spring to mind but nothing was quite like the Stoll. The Stoll had a niche market, it had to as in comparison to others it was rather run down and shoddy. It showed dirty films with an X certificate.

Joe Rogerson

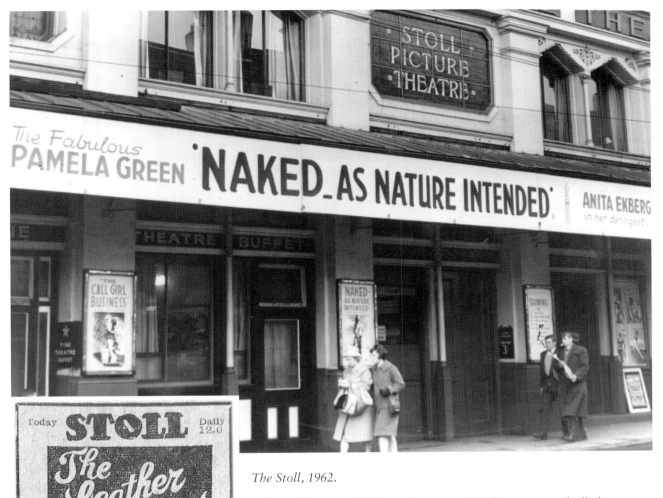

The Stoll, 1962.

'The Stoll attracted old men in macs and older testerone-fuelled teenagers and I can well remember going to see a film called 36 24 36 only to find, to my utmost disappointment, that it was the only musical ever shown there.' (Joe Rogerson)

The Apollo on Shields Road, Byker had its own enclosed car park and parking attendant. The manager in the 60s was David Hinge, son of North East theatre and cinema entrepreneur Edward Hinge. We would go to the Saturday children's matinee cartoons and silent comedies and serials such as *Flash Gordon* with Buster Crabbe. And we got tickets for the Christmas party with cartoons, games and a selection box for everyone.

The Queen's magnificent curved Cinerama screen, 1963.

We would sometimes go with Dad to the Saturday matinee at The Tatler cinema on Northumberland Street. It was a News Theatre with a long wide corridor showing posters of coming attractions, open to the street with the ticket kiosk at one corner. I remember the Pathe News Reel introduced by a crowing rooster.

We went to the Queen's cinema, the only cinema in the North East with the curved Cinerama screen. In 1968 I went to see *2001 a Space Odyssey* there, and remember the baffled comments from the other patrons as we left. In 1969 we went to see *Kes* at the Tyneside Film Theatre on Pilgrim Street (now the Tyneside cinema) which had re-opened in 1968.

Brian Thompson

We went to see The Beatles' *Hard Days Night* and *Help*, Cliff Richard in *The Young Ones* and *Summer Holiday*, James Bond – *From Russia With Love* and *Dr No*. These were considered quite daring! Once you had paid your money you could stay as long as you liked as the programme ran continuously. I well remember sitting through some films (plus supporting film, news and adverts) more than once. I wonder if we took sandwiches or just survived on chocolate?

Jane Boyd (nee Turnbull)

The Haymarket, 1966.

We went to the pictures at the Haymarket, Odeon and Essoldo, often queuing to get in. You could sit through the main feature film twice if you wanted to. Alan often had a doze on a Monday afternoon at the Haymarket pictures while I was at work at William Leech (Builders) on St James Street, then he would go and do a night shift at Vickers Armstrong on Scotswood Road. He lived at Leam Lane Estate, Gateshead, which seemed miles away from Heaton where I lived.

Beryl Turner

I'M GOING TO CHANGE THE WORLD

May Day 1960

May Day events were a great labour movement ritual. Members of its great sections, political, industrial and co-operative would turn out in droves and young socialists could indulge their artistic flair. From 7.30am on the morning of the procession, numerous enthusiasts would turn up outside the Newgate Street Co-op store to decorate the floats with elaborate, themed tableaux. There could be 20 of them. In 1960, the City Young Socialists' theme was 'Ban the Bomb.' They made a large Polaris missile from strong wire, bed sheets and some grey paint.

Councillor Doris Starkey, the march organiser in chief was a tremendous bundle of energy. She would scurry around giving orders; sending people into the Co-op haberdashery to get more ribbon; someone else to the garage to find out where the Coxlodge Women's Guild truck had got to; settling a dispute; responding to a message about a speaker for the final rally; organising pots of tea – but you could only have five minutes!

Sometime after noon the floats would make their way down to the assembly point outside the Central Station where they would form up behind the group of Labour dignitaries and the float carrying the May Queen and her attendants – often shivering in skimpy dresses.

Between each series of tableaux would be a brass band warming up for action. In 1960 there were bands from, Ellington, Woodhorn, Newbiggin and Lynemouth, and Pegswood collieries, and Wallsend shipyards and Blyth British Railways. The procession, growing to over 2,000 people would make its way through crowded streets to the City Hall for a rally, with speeches from figures like Nye Bevan, and in 1960, Harold Wilson, relayed to the crowds outside the hall. They would disperse around four o'clock and people would rush home to get into their glad rags for the May Day Dance in the evening at the Mayfair Ballroom where a figure such as Dan Smith would lead off with the May Queen.

There was also an annual open air meeting on the Moor, in June, at the start of the Hoppings, where some youths cut their speaking teeth and dealt incompetently with various hecklers including the League of Empire Loyalists. In 1960 the meeting was preceded by a Young Socialist march on the South African issue where the police and army had just killed African protesters at Sharpeville.

In the winter was the staid Labour Party Annual Dance at the Mayfair. Some youngsters did ballroom dancing and even took dancing lessons at places like Miss Newbiggin's Silver Swing ballroom dancing school on Shields Road. A lesson cost 1s 6d. However this was the critical cross over moment for the young between the foxtrot and the twist. The Labour Party had just painfully recognised it and a tiny corner of the evening's programme was turned over to wild cavorting.

John Charlton

The May Day march gets underway, 1960, passing Joseph Cowen's memorial on Westgate Road.

Young CND

I was a serious and politically aware youngster, involved in the movements of the time, including the Campaign for Nuclear Disarmament, the Young Socialists and the Anti-Apartheid Movement.

Our Young Socialist group met in the Newcastle North HQ, which was in Winchester Terrace, overlooking Summerhill Square. For a while I was secretary of the group, although not

North East CND marchers, 1960, passing Kensington tube station, London.

a very good one, and was responsible for writing the minutes and inviting speakers. Our local MP, Ted Short, later Lord Glenamara, once gave us a talk on Christian Socialism, perhaps not realising that a high proportion of the group was Jewish. Another speaker was Anthony Crosland, later a minister in Harold Wilson's government.

After meetings on a Sunday evening we would often walk down to the Bigg Market where there was a 'Speakers Corner' with both political and religious groups trying to persuade and recruit. We used to heckle some of them, which they relished because many of them were expert in the art of the witty riposte. The Communist Party was usually represented, and some fringe religious organisations like the Bethshan Tabernacle, who specialised in using very young children to buttonhole members of the audience and ask them if they had been saved in Christ.

The youth group of CND used to meet in the ILP (Independent Labour Party) Hall in Shields Road. Some of us were interested in writing poetry, so we started printing a magazine called 'Eruption', and were loosely allied with the poets who set up readings in the Morden Tower. I used to edit the magazine, and was responsible for turning down some poetry written by the council leader, T. Dan Smith, because I didn't think it was good enough quality! I must only have been about 16 at the time. Among the people who helped us with the magazine were C.P. Taylor and Basil Bunting, both well-known North East literary figures.

Editing the magazine was an education in typing stencils, which were almost impossible to correct. The stencils were then wound onto an old hand-operated Roneo machine. The machine was inked and you turned the handle to run off copies.

Fiona Clarke

At 16 I joined Newcastle Young CND. I became treasurer and Secretary. Here I met Tony Jackson, the beat poet. Tony worked with Tom Pickard in the Ultima Thule bookshop. He was arrested for reading Allan Ginsberg's controversial poem *Howl* in the Bigg Market one Sunday night, when Newcastle had its own version of Speakers' Corner. The cops took him away in a van.

YCND met in the YMCA next to the Palletta café and in pubs in the city. We fasted for three days at the Haymarket Monument protesting against the Vietnam War. We had protest marches around the city though there were rarely more than 30 of us altogether. We were usually booed and jeered at. Members of CND were also part of Newcastle's Anarchist, Communist and Socialist groups. We had 'wild' parties every weekend. Everybody met at the Haymarket at the Angel and off we would go to any party, invited or not.

After listening to a guest speaker who was a vegetarian I became one myself.

Malcolm Henderson

My school uniform consisted of bottle green skirt, blazer and burberry with red tie and white shirt, I believe there was a hat in there somewhere but I never saw anyone wearing it. It was pretty hard to customise it but we did our best, hitching skirts up to be minis or dropping them to the hips to be maxis and using the tie as a belt (never in our strict girls' school though) and in 1963 we thought we looked the bees knees. There was the option to wear a duffel coat instead of a Burberry and this is where we really went to town. It was the era of CND and 'ban the bomb' marches, which we were not allowed to attend, but we did our bit by chalking the CND sign and slogans onto the back of our coats. We used chalk in order to brush it off before we went home and our mothers saw it. However, one day we went to call for our friend Edna and Edna's mother invited us in to wait. She had just bought a new black moquette three piece suite and told us to try it out. Unfortunately, when we got up there were three perfect CND emblems imprinted on her new sofa. We left the house much more rapidly than we had entered and didn't call for Edna for quite some time.

June Sains

The Oxfam Walk, May 6,1967

I had just turned 20 and was working for Vickers Armstrong's on Scotswood Road – that is where I got most of my sponsor money for the walk. In those days sponsorship forms, never mind 26 mile walks, were very unusual.

Three of my friends – Joan Gibson, Pauline Wilson, Carol Smith – and I started the night off in Carter's Wine Lodge – The Ladies' Room that is – where we often went. There were no energy drinks, just Cherry B and cider and the odd barley wine. The owner let us stay until 11.30pm, then we made our way up to St James' for the midnight start.

I don't think there was anything like a track suit or a pair of trainers – in fact I wore a pair of stiletto slingbacks and a long black leather coat. Even then we had pride in our appearance! We were all carrying handbags and make-up. We had no idea what was to come. We also had no idea of the horrific drama that occurred when there was a false start and a girl of 17 was crushed to death.

We seemed to reach the Kenton Bar in next to no time and then down into Ponteland where there was a heavy mist – we all worried that our mascara would run! The first feeding station seemed like it was never coming – no wonder as it was 11 miles from the start. The night was never ending – especially when the alcohol wore off. We all then started to feel very cold and were contemplating hitching a lift home! But we didn't. That walk down Barrack Road to the finish was a killer. No medals at the end. We got a certificate in the post but unfortunately mine has long disappeared.

After waiting for ever for a bus and having problems getting on and off as my legs had seized up, I eventually got home. I immediately had a hot bath (my mam kept knocking on the bathroom door as she thought I had passed out with exhaustion). I tended to my blisters (of which there were many) and went to bed. Needless to say I didn't make it into work on the Monday – I think it was the first day's sick I had ever had. Never mind it was all in a good cause and I raised quite a bit of money.

Lynda Mason

8,000 hope to raise £6,000 for Oxfam

THE Oxfam Walk weather forecast: Cloudy and misty, with possible showers during the period of the walk.

Opposite, the Civic Centre nears completion, 1967.

CONCRETE AND CLAY

Dirty old town

When I arrived here in November 1964 I knew nothing of Newcastle. Men from Henley-on-Thames don't! I was taken to the Red House on the Sandhill and was fascinated by the cellars below and beamed rooms above. I was so impressed by those incredible bridges. It was close to Christmas and Sandhill was busy in contrast to the Quayside with its shipping offices enlivened only by the Baltic Tavern in Broad Chare. There was a pronounced absence of people in the evenings. There was nothing to attract people and, in the years before the interceptor sewer, every reason not to linger!

I recall evenings walking down the stairs of the Quayside Chares along to the New Sun Inn, complete with sawdust on its floor. It was quieter in those days. The area of Pandon, behind the Quayside, was special with its medieval street plan unchanged. It was a picture of quaintness with small businesses in Manor Chare operating amongst nearby decay. Newcastle then was an exciting place to explore.

Another special place was the Castle with its road going through the Black Gate right through to the old Northumberland County Court (now The Vermont Hotel). The road was all that remained of the 18th and 19th century tenement township that used to exist there. In the sixties, the Castle Garage Company had a small building there including a kiln shed covered with Russian vine.

Derelict buildings abounded. The Holy Jesus Hospital was left open to both the elements and the homeless. Hanover Street warehouses had incredibly exciting stairs, tunnelling through the buildings to emerge

Swan House, around 1968.

162

at the Close. Blackfriars, left to rot and probable demolition was seen as of no consequence and yet it was the largest remains of a Dominican friary in England even though its church was demolished in the 16th century to provide building stone.

Between the Cloth and the Groat Markets stood the Old Town Hall, derelict and eventually demolished, soot

A dreary Quayside, 1969. The Sunday Market was the only lively time.

coated, pigeon and starling decorated, another sad reminder of former glories of Newcastle, when every central street was packed with small businesses, shops and offices. Newcastle in the mid-60s was a blackened city with all its fabulous heritage of stone carrying thick encrustations of coal smoke deposits. It gave a generally depressing aspect and the later stone cleaning restored Newcastle to how Richard Grainger would have seen it.

The Grainger Market has survived essentially as it was in the sixties, but the adjoining wholesale vegetable market, which moved to the Team Valley, is a distant memory as are the fish market and a retail green market. This area was demolished to make way for the new Eldon Square shopping complex.

David Hughes

The town was full of old buildings, all dirty with decades of grime from coal fires and local industry. T. Dan Smith and his plans seemed a good idea at the time but we should have realised then that concrete was never going to be the answer. The Quayside was a desolate wasteland of empty dilapidated warehouses sheds and rail tracks. No one visited it except for the Sunday Market with its sarsaparilla and jumping beans sellers. St James' was no better, leaving aside the football, the least said the better about the ground.

Joe Rogerson

The city centre seemed a long way away from Byker, where I lived, and all of the stone buildings were black from years of air pollution. Many attractive buildings were pulled down in the name of progress when it would have been better to have cleaned them and refurbished the interiors. It breaks my heart to look at the Eldon Square of today and remember its fine predecessor.

Nick Rogerson

Eldon Square, 1965, a few years before the demolition of the North and West sides.

New Bridge Street in 1967. The blackened stones of the old Central Library would soon be knocked down to make way for John Dobson Street. The new Central Library, under construction, will take its place. Two churches have been demolished on New Bridge Street, which, before the Central Motorway East cut its concrete canyons through the city, snaked east to join Byker Bridge and eventually Shields Road.

The chewing gum sculpture

In the late 60s a controversial sculpture was bolted to the wall of the Laing Art Gallery, probably one of the first pieces of modern public art in Newcastle. People did not know if it was supposed to be a piece of red, white and yellow chewing gum stretching from the ground up the wall or liquid flowing out of the wall, I seem to remember I liked it but whether I was old enough to appreciate its aesthetic, probably not. It was definitely of its time but it was not allowed to stay long because of the public outcry it caused.

Brian Thompson

Like a monster from Dr Who, this strange sculpture appeared on the wall of the Laing soon after John Dobson Street was opened in 1969. The new Central Library beyond included a first floor entrance on the concrete deck.

I never had anything against the Civic Centre, but some awful buildings were put up in 60s – the Pearl Assurance building, and John Dobson Street. Real vandalism, but enough good stuff survived.

John Steel

The tower seemed to go on up forever with finally the three castles, and sea horses around the bell chamber of the carillon.

David Hughes

Above, the foundation stone ceremony, Civic Centre, 1960.

Right, the 12 storey office block was complete by 1966. The whole complex was formally opened by King Olav of Norway on 14 November, 1968.

By the end of the 1960s a wedding dress might be extremely mini, and nobody would bat an eye! The bride is on the right.

Opposite, Maureen Brook's wedding, 24 February, 1962 (Maureen Brook).

I GOT YOU BABE

The Wedding

We were married at 3pm on 24th February, 1962: a cold, grey day with sleety showers. It was not a grand wedding, by any means, for our finances were extremely tight and the fashion for elaborate weddings had not yet gathered pace. The venue was St Vincent's RC church in Walker. It was a 'mixed marriage' in that I was a Roman Catholic and my husband-to-be, Fred, was a member of the Church of England. He was from Lancashire where, apparently, such weddings were less frequent. Over the previous nine months of our engagement he had faced the question, 'Are you turning then?' many times.

We'd met at a dance at the Old Assembly Rooms just one year and one week previously. He was in his second year of teaching at Hexham Grammar School and I was a personal assistant to a buyer at F.W. Reddaway in Walker, a subsidiary of George Angus, which made fire-fighting equipment.

When we married he was just short of his 26th birthday, having spent three years at university in London, followed by two years of National Service in Germany and then another year doing a teaching diploma at Newcastle University. I was 20 and had done low-paid clerical work since I was 15.

We were from similar working class families – his father had been a cotton spinner and mine was an electrician. Fred's father was suffering from terminal cancer and my father was unable to work because of a severe heart condition. This meant that neither family had money available for a 'big bash', so if we were to be wed, we had to find the finances from our very limited means.

My dress, ballerina length in white nylon lace with cap sleeves and a princess-line bodice, was an absolute bargain from the sale rail at C & A's on Northumberland Street and cost 30 shillings. Lillian, my mother-in-law, later told me that hers had cost five times as much in 1932. My veil was borrowed from a work colleague, as was the tiara that accompanied it. The most expensive item I bought were my shoes (not a surprise, says Fred, who knows all about my fondness for shoes). They cost the mighty sum of £3 from Dolcis in Grainger Street and were white, pearlised stiletto heels, very much in fashion at the time.

My bridesmaids were my two sisters, Anne, just a year younger than me, wearing a dress of figured nylon in her favourite colour, lilac. Not my choice, but since she was paying for her own dress, what could I say? My other sister, Teresa, who was just six, wore a lemon, nylon party dress I had bought. She loved it and wore it to everything until it was outgrown. We also had a page boy, my youngest brother, aged four, in white shorts, socks and pullover and a red tie. He claims he has never looked so smart since then.

Our best man was an ex-army friend of Fred's, originally from Yorkshire but working at the time in Gateshead. The priest who officiated was the delightful Father James Colgan. Because Fred was not Roman Catholic we had been obliged to agree to 'instruction' in the Catholic faith – a series of weekly

Fenwick, Newcastle

Fenwick's wedding fashions, around 1968. Dresses from here might cost a bit more than 30 shillings.

talks with the priest, lasting about eight or ten weeks. These turned out to be great fun. We know that Father Colgan enjoyed himself for, although we had forgotten to arrange for flowers or organist in the church, he had not, and paid for them out of his own pocket as a gift to us. This was just one of the many entirely uncalled for generosities we experienced.

My Aunt Sally, a florist in the Grainger Market, provided all the wedding bouquets and buttonholes absolutely free of charge. After I collected them, I flagged down a taxi – the first I had ever taken – to deliver them to the hotel where my in-laws and relatives were staying. The taxi driver then delivered me back to my digs in Walker but refused to take any fare, simply commenting, 'Have a lovely day tomorrow and a great life together.' It still moves me to tears when I think of this complete stranger's generosity. I hope that he, too, had a good life.

Thelma, one of my colleagues from work, offered the use of her house to me and my sisters to get ready for the wedding and we left from there for the church. It was a small gathering of family, friends and colleagues.

As a matter of courtesy, we had sent an invitation to my 90 year old Great-Aunt Nellie, from Riding Mill, who had not attended a family wedding in forty years. For some unknown reason, she chose to attend ours. Arriving late, she stormed up the aisle, dyed red hair blazing, waving her walking stick and complaining that there had been no taxi to meet her at the railway station – naturally so, since we weren't aware that she was coming. The imperturbable Father Colgan allowed her to settle herself before continuing with the simple wedding service.

After the ceremony, we filed outside to be met with a sleet storm. The photographer did his best, but it's difficult to get decent photos when your subjects are clinging together and shivering and, remember, my dress had cap sleeves!

As the neighbouring children hovered expectantly by the church gates, my elder brother returned to the church, scooped up the pile of coppers he'd placed on a cap on the radiators and performed the 'Hoyin' Oot' as we got into his car. My new husband was baffled by this strange ceremony.

The reception was at the Co-operative Hall in Raby Street, Byker where three elderly Nora Battys served us with a buffet meal and pointed out that our Best Man – always a man for the ladies – was chatting up the girls rather than seeing to the guests. A little later we left to get changed at Thelma's house to their chorus of 'Ee, what a lovely couple and, you knaa, she's not even pregnant!' My going-away outfit was a navy Italian jersey suit which cost more than my wedding dress, even though second-hand.

When we returned, our best man had secured his date, but all our other guests had drifted back into embarrassed groups, without finding a way of introducing themselves to one another. Hard work by us, and the rest of the champagne – the real stuff, we knew our priorities even then – did wonders for them.

There was no honeymoon. Every penny we had available had been put towards the deposit on a terraced house of our own in Tynedale or on the wedding itself, so it was back to our new home to unwrap the wedding presents which included four candlewick bedspreads, three sets of sheets, one pillow. Um … we'd forgotten to buy blankets and pillows for ourselves. So, we snuggled down under the candlewick bedspreads, head to head on the one pillow. We're still together, 47 years on.

Maureen Brook

The price of love

I married my first wife, Karina, on July 8th, 1963, at St Theresa's Church, Heaton. I still have the bill for our wedding reception. The prices seem astonishing today – 25 luncheons for £16 17s 6d, and 6 bottles of Sauternes for £5 8s! The reception was held at Club Astor, which was attached to the People's Theatre on Stephenson Road.

Karina was German and we met while I was on National Service. I was among the last to be called up (in October 1960) before National Service ended in December 1960.

Mike Jamieson

After three years of courting, we decided to get engaged. Alan got permission from my dad and bought the ring from H. Samuel on Northumberland Street. My parents needed two years to save up for the wedding and we needed two years to save up for a mortgage. Most people just rented property.

I started a 'bottom drawer' with towels and stainless steel items (the new 'in' thing). We bought teak furniture, candlewick bedspreads, goatskin rugs, an electric wringer, and a washing machine for our upstairs flat (which had no inside toilet, only one in the back yard). The downstairs flat was ours too and was rented by two old gentlemen. You bought flats in pairs then.

We bought a dining room suite at the Co-op, paying for it in weekly instalments. HP (hire purchase) was the way to buy goods we couldn't afford – there were no offers of credit cards then. I won a fridge in an *Evening Chronicle* competition when I was 17 so we had that for our new flat. We rented our TV from DER and paid weekly for it at the offices in Higham Place. A telephone came later on as did a twin tub

Mike Jamieson

MONTHLY STATEMENT

Club Astor

STEPHENSON ROAD · NEWCASTLE UPON TYNE 6
Tel. 65-5978

Name Mrs. Jamieson,

Address 63 Rokeby Terrace,

Newcastle upon Tyne, 6.

TPW 31841 WEDDING RECEPTION, 8th. July. 1963.

	To Goods.			
25	Luncheons	16	17	6
2	Children	1	–	–
32	Ammontillado Sherry	4	–	–
6	Bottles Sauternes	5	8	–
12	Whiskies	1	10	–
4	Orange		4	–
		28	19	6
	15% Service Charge	4	7	–
	Hire of Hall	2	2	–
	Flowers & Decoration	2	–	–
	£	37	8	6.

washer. Big bold colours for wallpaper were in fashion and I remember having a very hard job trying to buy red emulsion paint!

Our wedding day arrived. Our wedding photographs (in black and white, no colour) were taken by Searle & O'Rourke who were just starting then. Hairstyles were changing, blow-drying was coming in and Bobby styled my hair. My wedding dress was made by a well-known dressmaker in High Bridge.

Two years passed and the time came for us to try for a baby. I fell pregnant in 1968 and left work as a secretary at Tyne Tees Television when I was six months pregnant. I couldn't go back to work after our son was born as jobs weren't kept open for you then.

We saw the first man to walk on the Moon in 1969 and felt was that life was quickly changing. New technology was being invented; we now had a telephone and plans were drawn up to have an inside toilet installed (no more cold trips down the back stairs to use the outside one!).

Beryl Turner

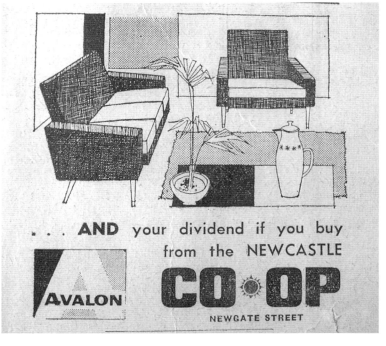

. . . AND your dividend if you buy from the NEWCASTLE **CO·OP** NEWGATE STREET

AVALON

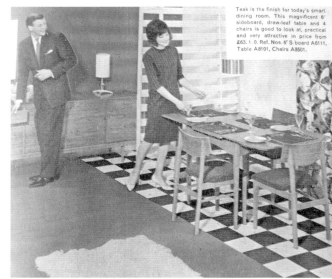

Teak is the finish for today's smart dining room. This magnificent 6' sideboard, draw-leaf table and 4 chairs is good to look at, practical and very attractive in price from £63.1.0. Ref. Nos. 6' S.board A6111, Table A8101, Chairs A8501.

DANGER
SEVERE RAMP

SINGLE LANE
TRAFFIC AHEAD

WONDERFUL LAND

The view from the South

I spent my teenage years in North Yorkshire, just 40 miles from Newcastle, but after crossing the Tyne Bridge in 1968 it was as if I was in another country. What a sweet and sour culture shock – everything from chips with everything to Newcastle Brown. But it wasn't just what people put into their mouths so much as what came out. I just couldn't understand Geordie, despite my own northern links. This was a big problem because I'd come to Newcastle to work on *The Journal*. Reporters are supposed to get people to open up and talk, not say repeatedly: 'I'm very sorry – but … just … what did you say?

One old Geordie asked where I came from. 'North Yorkshire, just an hour down the A1,' I replied. Pausing for a few seconds, he looked me up and down, and from back to front, and said: 'Oh, the south?'

What did I think of Tyneside, he wanted to know. (Everyone wanted to know.) Best not, I thought, to say anything about 'a foreign country'. The people, I said, were very friendly and welcoming – which was true – the sweet part of the culture shock. He bought me a beer, as did a lot of other people.

My then girlfriend, Pat, a fellow *Journal* reporter from Essex, was bowled over by Tyneside warmth. She exclaimed in our first week: 'Everyone here seems to know my name!'…Well, actually, the truth is she didn't know her 'Pet' from her 'Pat'.

We had our own favourite Geordie words such as 'Filoom' (film) or should it have been 'Fillum'? We practised them, very quietly so no-one could hear, while walking to catch the 33 bus from Jesmond down past the new Civic Centre to the Central Station. Yes, we lived in the posh part of town, within reach of smelly Jesmond Dene.

I'd come to Newcastle from the green posh of Letchworth Garden City, 35 miles north of London. Letchworth was full of leafy wide open spaces; Newcastle full of black. There was black on the window sill, black in the bathroom, black on my shirts even though the landlady could have won national awards for being house-proud.

And then there were the deep black eyes of Felling. Letchworth council meetings were polite, sober affairs. My first Felling Council meeting ended with a council chamber punch up – elected councillors actually trading blows. I called the *Journal* news-desk with this big story – to be greeted with total indifference. Was this kind of fracas so common in this strange land, I wondered, that it wasn't even worth reporting? It would have been front page in Letchworth, big and bold.

But I owe a lot to this strange land – and best of all, a wife, also from posh Jesmond.

John Illman

I arrived in Newcastle in autumn 1965 as a graphic design student at the College of Art & Industrial Design. For the first term I had lodgings in Allendale Road, and attended college mainly in Chillingham Road. 'Old Byker' was my first experience of the city.

In November, one Saturday it snowed. I decided to take my camera and walk into town. I didn't realise then that my subject matter was soon to disappear.

First to go were the yellow trolleybuses, in the late spring of 1966. These used to glide almost silently up and down Shields Road, past Parrish's department store with its plastic money, (I understand old Byker residents used to 'deal' in Parrish's money) and over Byker Bridge, with impressive gantries of poles and wires. Meanwhile, early Leyland Atlanteans on the No 12 route proclaimed their cross-city destination: Two Ball Lonnen.

Other memories of student life at that time involved long coffee breaks at the back of Mark Toney's in Grainger Street, lunches in Fenwick's Patio Bar and a meal at an early Chinese restaurant in the basement of Emerson Chambers. We searched the old Bainbridge's delicatessen in Market Street for green peppers. We also bought a strange cheese called Brie and were surprised when it melted all over the plate!

Charles Soulby

The number 12 climbs Commercial Road, Byker, 1960s. St Peter's is on the right. Byker's steep slopes, panoramic views over the city, and long dark terraces of Tyneside flats with characteristically 'stepped' rooflines, combined to create a unique urban landscape that could only be Newcastle.

My first visit to Newcastle was in the autumn of 1961. I arrived at Central Station with my mother, who was requested to attend an interview with me at the RVI. I was accepted by the matron, Miss Freda Shaw and started as a cadet in January 1962. Nurse training began in June when I was 18. Framlington Place was home for the next three months – in between lectures, meals consisted of meat and two veg followed by rhubarb and custard!

After that stage, our crowd moved into the Nurses' Home and work started on the wards. Every 12 weeks we moved to different departments to gain experience in various disciplines. I disliked night duty but loved being at the babies' hospital in Leazes Terrace.

The city came as a culture shock compared with my home town, Middlesbrough. Everything was so vibrant, magnificent buildings, wonderful shops, theatres, cinemas, restaurants – just a great place to be.

As nurses, we were given privileges which included the use of the Royal Grammar School swimming baths. There were free tickets to shows, and glamourous Yana signed autographs for us. An invitation to a performance by Northern Sinfonia Orchestra with a young Canadian conductor was memorable. He'd been a patient and wished to show his gratitude.

After a year and having passed preliminary exams, we were allowed to move from the constraints of the nurse's home into rented accommodation. Four of us shared a flat in Newlands Road, High West Jesmond.

Rosemary Dane

My boyfriend, later husband, was car mad. Days off were spent visiting garages including Northern Motors in Byker looking at engines, leather front bench seats, and gear sticks on steering wheels. He had a green and cream Ford Zodiac, followed by a black Zephyr and finally a Speedwell Blue Austin Healey Sprite. This model was known as the 'Friendly Frog'

I passed my final exams in July 1965 and became a State Registered Nurse. Marriage followed, and having to stock up the kitchen from scratch. Bainbridge's supplied and delivered vast amounts of groceries all for £10. They had a fabulous food section. Furniture was purchased from Callers, Ercol was the 'in thing'. Our three children were born at the Princess Mary Maternity Hospital. The registrar visited to record births when my daughter was born in 1966 but by 1969, when my second child arrived, I had to register his birth at the new Civic Centre.

Rosemary Dane

Central Station, 1967, no continental piazza.

Mellow Yellow

I arrived in Newcastle at the end of the 1960s to start work. I'd come from a small town, where M&S was the sole fashion outlet, clad in duffle-coat and sensible shoes, so I was immediately stunned by sophisticated city life!

I stayed at first at the YWCA in Saville Place and travelled to work on the distinctive yellow double-decker that I caught off Northumberland Street. In fact yellow seemed to be the colour of the late 60s. I remember buying a yellow crepe shirt from Fenwick's. Fenwick's was the place for clothes … when you could afford it. I stepped out confidently for the bus each morning, feeling so trendy in my Fenwick's tweed coat, jumper and mini skirt, with yellow knee-length socks and black patent shoes.

Perhaps we needed the colour in Newcastle in those days. Central Newcastle was shabby … the old, well-loved buildings had yet to be sand-blasted. The Central Station was no continental piazza. When I occasionally stopped there for Sunday lunch (in between Elswick and Jesmond) I would go for a comforting hot meat pie and mushy peas at the Station Café. Italian-style coffee houses hadn't arrived. The only bit of 'foreign' was Mark Toney's in Grainger Street.

I coveted a bright orange dress that I saw every day in the window of BHS as I passed it on the bus. A boyfriend eventually bought it for me. It was my dream dress and I wore it and wore it! Etam's was another trendy store … I loved the gorgeous colours and fabrics. C & A was my favourite place for buying run-of-the-mill clothes.

I adored Handyside Arcade and still mourn its passing. It felt slightly daring and decadent to go shopping there, with its 19th century wrought-iron work and puddles where the roof leaked. Fascinating small shops sold Indian sandals, joss sticks, jewellery and 'Lord of the Rings' posters.

Bainbridge was then in Market Street and the place to go if your income necessitated making everything by hand. I bought my first blanket there (yellow), material for my first pair of curtains (a bold pattern of pink, orange and blue) and endless lampshade frames for my artistic attempts with raffia.

Rose Reeve

The 1960s was the most exciting decade of my life. I discovered that the best thing about Middlesbrough was the road out of it to Newcastle!

Rosemary Dane

Traffic, and a whole fleet of yellow buses, clogs Northumberland Street, Christmas, mid-1960s (Charles Soulby).

Newcastle's Christmas Blaze

Fenwick's Christmas window is a Newcastle tradition that dates back for decades. In the 1960s other stores used animated displays to attract Christmas shoppers. One was furniture store, Callers, which had arcade windows leading back from the facade on Northumberland Street.

Callers' Christmas display 1969 very nearly caused the destruction of the entire city centre. On the evening of Sunday 30th November, the usual crowds of excited children and parents had turned out to see Callers' attractive and magical animated Dickensian-themed display. However, one sharp-eyed father, his mental faculties not yet fully smothered by the demands of the festive period or an excess of cheap sherry, found his attention drawn to a thin plume of smoke rising gently from the head of a mechanical street urchin, and rushed to a nearby telephone box to alert the fire service.

Within a few minutes the entire display, built mostly of papier-maché and polystyrene, was alight, the flames being helped along nicely by the electric fans powering the toy windmills decorating the ceiling of the store's arcade entrance. The fire quickly took hold, spreading throughout the shop and into the building's upper floors by the time Newcastle & Gateshead Fire Service arrived. They could do nothing to save the building, but their efforts were vital in ensuring the flames did not spread any further, or leap across the road to the other side of Northumberland Street, which would have been disastrous. 88 firefighters using 15 appliances struggled for five hours to bring the blaze under control, and it took another four to extinguish the conflagration using high expansion foam.

This was the worst fire seen in Newcastle's city centre, causing upwards of two million pounds worth of damage. Callers and the adjacent Van Allan and Richard shops were completely gutted. After inspection, the building facade was declared unsafe, and demolished shortly afterwards. Miraculously, only three people were injured – including Leading Fireman Harry Louvre, commended for his bravery, who continued to fight the blaze for four hours after sustaining severe burns to the hands and face.

Staff at Tyne & Wear Archives & Museums

Callers burns, 30 November, 1969. People watched from the Northumberland Arms opposite. This fire engine tackles the blaze from Saville Row.

183

ON A CAROUSEL

The Hoppings

We arrive at the Town Moor bus terminal, at the southern end of the show ground, with its usual queue of trolley buses, spewing passengers out by the score. A hardly discernible, bluish, grey haze hangs in the air, enveloping the fairground in the sweet, sickly scent of burning diesel fuel.

Ears are assaulted by the low throb of indestructible Gardener and Perkin's Diesel Engines, as they drone on with a slow melodic rhythm, never skipping a beat, whilst churning out hundreds of volts of electricity and driving the machines effortlessly.

The tarry smell of coal burning, as it powers the ancient steam engines that many travellers still love, and petrol fumes from the cars in the traffic jam that runs the full length of the fair ground from its southern to northern limits. It is the second last week in June 1960 and the largest travelling fair in the world is here again.

The Hoppings is a truly magical place for us all, an Aladdin's cave of goodies and boundless possibilities from fortune tellers and touts (who offer a range of ways to part with our cash in exchange for the 'promise' of a prize or experiencing the ride of a lifetime).

Hundreds of people of all ages wait patiently for the Lord Mayor, dressed in full regalia, to perform the official opening. Rock and roll music plays from the wildest rides, and a mix of ballads and country music, by artists such as Dicky Valentine, Slim Whitman and Tommy Steele, comes from the myriad of side shows.

A Rolls Royce pulls up at the gate and the police clear a pathway to a pedestal near the entrance. The show men switch their sound systems off, there is a hush as the Mayor leaves the car with the mace and sword bearers following a pace or so behind. People move to get a better view of the procession, men doff their caps and women tell impatient children to be quiet and settle. There are slaps and cries for children who find it difficult to do as they are told.

A short speech later, the snip of scissors, and the Hoppings snaps into life. Vendors cry out loudly, trying to sell desirable objects such as balloons, goldfish, masks of cartoon characters and cheap toys from well-laden barrows, large cases and small static booths.

Finally free, the children tug at their parents' clothing and beg for ice creams, toys and a go on the rides. There is so much happening, it is difficult to know where to start in those few acres of meadow.

It was unforgettable!

Joseph J Robson

Bernie Ramamandi

By the time we were teenagers we looked forward to The Hoppings every June. It did tend to get in the way of exams in later years but where I lived you heard the sound of the fair and the smell the of onions and candy floss drifted across the Town Moor. Even though there were some rough looking blokes hanging about we certainly never felt anything but happy just being there. We would go most nights even without any money, just for the atmosphere.

Mik Richardson

Central Library, 1967. In 1968 the Victorian building closed its doors and the new concrete Central Library opened.

Opposite, the main door to Newcastle's new Central Library, 1970.

MY LITTLE RED BOOK

The Central Library, old and new

I remember the old Central Library with its great stone pillared entrance on New Bridge Street. Next to the library was a small grassed area, where a tramp regularly sat on one of the benches, smiling at passers by, and further west was Broughs the Grocers, and City Stylish menswear shop as well as the greasy spoon café. Opposite was the Dex Garage and next to the Dex entrance was the fruit'n'veg barrow man who was always busy.

Barry and Ida Dobson

The old library was Victorian, a narrow oblong room which incorporated the Newcastle Mechanics Institute library of the 1850s. The main building had an imposing facade of stone carvings (some of these are now built into the walls of the Eldon Square shopping centre).

It was difficult to work in. It was too small for a start and it was on different levels. You couldn't use a book trolley. Everything had to be carried by hand. We must have been fit, going up and down ladders and carrying everything. I remember the City Librarian, Mr Tynemouth, used to say 'there is no such thing as light literature when it's carried in bulk.'

Detached from the library was an annex, an unlovely square building. It was devoted to newspapers, which were on the ground floor. The papers were on slopes with the betting news blacked out. We were real spoilsports. We'd also lace the current newspapers onto boards so that people couldn't take them away. Heavy bound volumes of newspapers were in the basement. If someone wanted a bound volume of newspapers you'd have to go to this building and carry it back.

In the 1960s the city decided to redesign the road system to relieve traffic. The library stood right in the way of the proposed John Dobson Street so it had to come down. Suddenly we were told we were getting a new library. Mr Tynemouth planned it and the architects were astounded. They said it was one of the best library briefs they'd ever had.

The Sir Basil Spence team got involved because the council said they wanted the leading architect of the day. He agreed, but he was involved in some major project in India at the time so he delegated the work to his Edinburgh office. He approved the plans they made but he never came to visit the site or even visited the committee so no one ever got to actually meet him and they felt snubbed! Some people did comment that it was a very austere Scottish building built by Scottish architects.

When we opened we were really busy and we were very pleased with the new building. We found ourselves in a well-designed library with plenty of space and very good staffing facilities.

There were huge queues to get in as well as queues for both the in and out counters. Life became dominated by Catherine Cookson; we could never buy sufficient copies of her books. We used to buy about 100 copies of each new book and some readers would still have to wait a year before they could read it, which they were quite happy to do as no one in those days bought books.

Arthur Wallace (Librarian)

I wrote to the City Librarian, Mr Tynemouth, asking for a job. I was invited for interview and given a job on the spot! I started in September 1967 in the beautiful 85-year-old building in New Bridge Street. I well remember the queues on a Saturday morning along New Bridge Street, even stretching to Cook's Corner, if some reader's tickets couldn't be found in those rows and rows of wooden trays!

Other memories include clambering along on hands and knees to retrieve books from a nook or cranny and climbing out of the staff room window to sunbathe on a section of the roof overlooking the Laing.

After six months I was moved to the Reference Library with its magnificent

Central Library, 1967.

half-circle reading room where assistants had to climb up tall ladders to retrieve material. With the advent of mini-skirts, we were soon allowed to wear 'trouser suits' – no jeans or T-shirts in those days.

Gail Richardson

My trip into town that November Saturday ended in the warmth of the new Central Library – an impression of grey concrete with hairy carpets. After the essentially Victorian library in my home town it seemed positively 'state of the art'. At that time, T. Dan Smith was promoting his vision of Newcastle as the 'new Brasilia', although the A1 still went up Northumberland Street and most of the buildings were black.

Charles Soulby

When the new Central Library opened in 1968 I was doing A levels and it was a great place to study, but, more important, lots of other sixth formers went there. The boys from Rutherford had some very useful notes! The study rooms on the second floor were patrolled by peaked-capped janitors who tried to stop us talking. Soon it would be time to go downstairs to Princess Square and the Man in the Moon. We seemed to get into that pub with no problem.

Anna Flowers

I remember when the new library was built, it was very impressive, we used to get our No 12 bus outside there, snogging a couple of boys at the same time, I may add.

Karin Musson

Opposite, so much had changed – the city centre in 1968. The Civic Centre is complete. John Dobson Street, the Central Library and Swan House (bottom right) are brand new. Eldon Square awaits demolition. The Polytechnic is expanding. (TWAM / Turners)